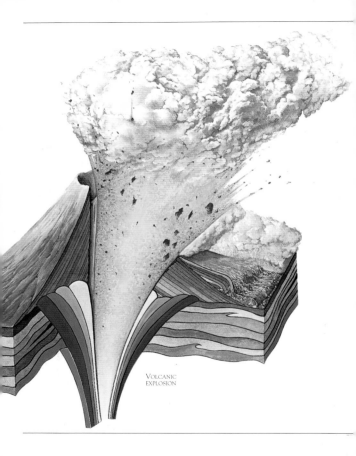

VOLCANIC
EXPLOSION

P · O · C · K · E · T · S

VOLCANOES

Written by
JOHN FARNDON

VOLCANIC TUFF

EARTH'S TECTONIC PLATES

CHARRED
HUMAN
BONE FROM
POMPEII

VOLCANIC CINDERS AND LAPILLI

LAYERS OF
VOLCANIC ASH

DORLING KINDERSLEY
London • New York • Moscow • Sydney

A DORLING KINDERSLEY BOOK

Produced for Dorling Kindersley by
PAGE*One*, Cairn House, Elgiva Lane, Chesham,
Buckinghamshire HP5 2JD

Project directors Bob Gordon, Helen Parker
Editor Sophie Williams
Art editor Thomas Keenes

DK team Jayne Parsons, Gill Shaw, Maggie Crowley
Production Joanne Rooke
Picture research Sally Hamilton, Deborah Pownall
Jacket design Dean Price

Published in Great Britain by
Dorling Kindersley Limited, 9 Henrietta Street,
London WC2E 8PS

2 4 6 8 10 9 7 5 3 1

A CIP catalogue record for this book is available from
the British Library.

ISBN 0-7513-5822-3

Colour reproduction by Colourscan, Singapore
Printed and bound in Italy by L.E.G.O.

Contents

HOW TO USE THIS BOOK

THESE PAGES show you how to use *Pockets: Volcanoes*. The book is divided into five sections, which explain how, why, and where volcanoes erupt, and earthquakes occur. There is also an introductory section and a fact-filled reference section. Each section begins with a picture page and a contents list.

HEADING AND INTRODUCTION
These provide an overview of the subject, to help you understand what the pages are about. Within the section, each page begins a new aspect of the subject.

RUNNING HEADS
These remind you which section you are in. The top of the left-hand page gives the section name. The top of the right-hand page gives the subject.

Corner coding   Running head

EFFUSIVE VOLCANOES

MANY VOLCANOES do not explode violently, but ooze lava almost continuously. These effusive, or flowing, volcanoes occur where the magma is fairly runny and low in gas. In basaltic magma like this, the gases have time to leak out before it reaches the surface. So the lava sprays out of the ground in a fountain of fire, or wells out as a stream of molten rock.

When pahoehoe reaches the sea, it settles gently into the water.

PAHOEHOE LAVA
Effusive volcanoes produce two types of lava, known by their Hawaiian names of pahoehoe and aa. Pahoehoe is hot, runny lava that flows freely. As its surface cools it forms a wrinkled, rope-like skin. Pahoehoe typically comes forward in shallow, tongue-like flows, moving at about 1 in (30) a minute.

AA LAVA
When lava fountains spray molten rock into the air, it cools and clots as it falls. This creates a crumbly, lumpy lava called aa. Aa shuffles forward on steep, folding over itself like a bulldozer track.

Lithosphere

CORNER CODING
The corners of the pages in each section are colour-coded as follows to remind you which section you are in.

▪ VOLCANIC ERUPTIONS
▪ VOLCANIC DISASTERS
▪ VOLCANOES AND THE ENVIRONMENT
▪ VOLCANIC PRODUCTS
▪ EARTHQUAKES

Introduction

Caption

LABELS
For extra clarity, some pictures have labels. They may give extra information, or identify a picture when it is not obvious from the text what it is.

FACTBOX

Many pages have tinted fact boxes, which provide extra points of information related to the subject dealt with on that page. The fact box shown on the page below contains facts about basalt lava.

REFERENCE SECTION

The reference section pages are yellow and are found at the back of the book. On these, you will find interesting facts and information, such as the myths and superstitions surrounding volcanoes and earthquakes.

Heading

Fact box

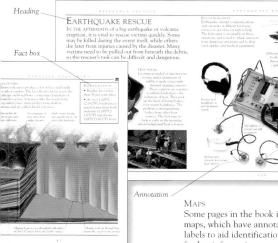

Annotation

MAPS

Some pages in the book include maps, which have annotations and labels to aid identification and give further information.

CAPTIONS AND ANNOTATIONS

Each illustration or photograph has an explanatory caption. Some also have annotations in *italics*. These are usually accompanied by leader lines, and can point out the features of an illustration.

INDEX AND GLOSSARY

At the back of the book you will find an index that alphabetically lists subjects included in the book, and a useful glossary to help you understand the terms used in each section.

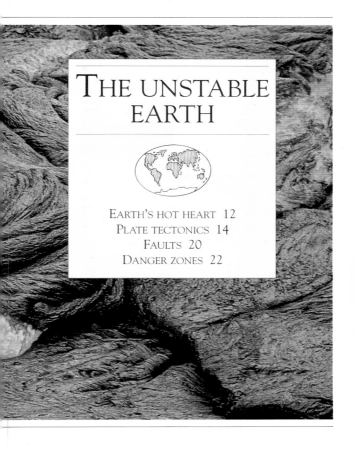

THE UNSTABLE EARTH

EARTH'S HOT HEART

THE EARTH IS not as solid as it seems. Less than 70 kilometres (43 miles) below our feet, Earth's fiery interior, or mantle, is hot enough to make rock flow like treacle. The mantle churns slowly with a power that can make the ground tremble, force volcanoes to erupt, and cause continents to collide.

THIN-SKINNED
The Earth's crust, when compared to its diameter of 12,750 km (7,927 miles), is as thin as an apple's skin. At its thickest, the crust is just 70 km (43 miles) deep.

PERIDOTITE

MANTLE ROCK
From under the crust, the Earth's mantle extends 2,900 km (1,800 miles) deep into the planet's interior. It is thought to be partly made of peridotite, a rock sometimes thrown up on to the surface during volcanic eruptions. The mantle is so hot that rock flows constantly, and in places actually melts altogether.

Meteorites from space are made of iron and nickel.

METAL CORE
The Earth has a dense core of iron, with a little nickel mixed in. Scientists know it is dense because it deflects earthquake waves. They believe it is iron and nickel because this is what meteorites are made from.

METEORITE

INSIDE THE EARTH

The complex structure of the Earth's interior was discovered by analyzing vibrations from earthquakes and volcanoes, which revealed a crust, mantle, and core. The crust and upper mantle are split into three layers: the rigid lithosphere, the weak asthenosphere, and the mesosphere.

HOT EARTH FACTS

• Mantle temperatures vary from 1,400°C (2,552°F) near the crust to 2,500°C (4,532°F) at the core.

• Core temperatures can rise to 3,700°C (6,662°F).

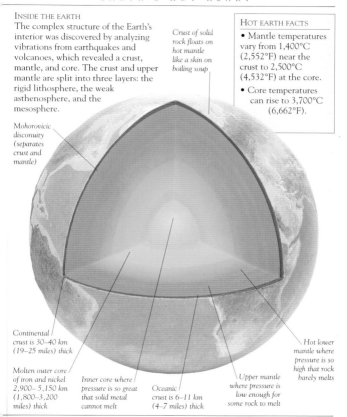

Crust of solid rock floats on hot mantle like a skin on boiling soup

Mohorovicic disconuity (separates crust and mantle)

Continental crust is 30–40 km (19–25 miles) thick

Molten outer core of iron and nickel 2,900–5,150 km (1,800–3,200 miles) thick

Inner core where pressure is so great that solid metal cannot melt

Oceanic crust is 6–11 km (4–7 miles) thick

Upper mantle where pressure is low enough for some rock to melt

Hot lower mantle where pressure is so high that rock barely melts

PLATE TECTONICS

THE EARTH'S RIGID shell, or lithosphere, is broken into huge fragments called tectonic plates. These plates are not fixed, but are continually moving on top of the mantle. In some places, plates are colliding (convergence zones); in others they are pulling apart (divergence zones); and in others they slide past each other (transforms).

Tectonic plates "float" on the mantle

Mantle

THE BROKEN SHELL
Earth's shell is made up of nine large tectonic plates and several smaller ones. Some plates are growing, while others are being worn away and will eventually disappear.

CONTINENTAL DRIFT

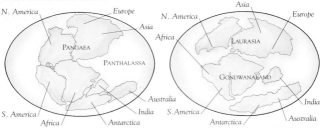

N. America   Europe
Asia
Africa
PANGAEA
PANTHALASSA
Australia
S. America   India
Africa   Antarctica

Asia
N. America   Europe
Africa
LAURASIA
GONDWANALAND
India
S.America   Australia
Antarctica

1 About 220 million years ago, all the continents were joined in the supercontinent of Pangaea, a Greek word meaning "all lands". Pangaea was surrounded by the giant ocean of Panthalassa, or "all seas".

2 By 200 million years ago, Pangaea had split into two huge landmasses called Laurasia and Gondwanaland. About 135 million years ago, these landmasses also began to divide, opening up what are now the world's oceans and seas.

MOVEMENT OF THE EARTH'S PLATES			
PLATE NAMES	DIRECTION OF MOVEMENT	RATE OF MOVEMENT	
		CM PER YEAR	IN PER YEAR
Pacific/Nazca	apart	18.3	7.3
Cocos/Pacific	apart	11.7	4.6
Nazca/South American	together	11.2	4.4
Pacific/Indo-Australian	together	10.5	4.1
Pacific/Antarctic	apart	10.3	4.0

PLATE MOVEMENT
Tectonic plates move very
slowly, drifting at about the
same rate as a fingernail
grows. Using laser and
satellite technology,
scientists can accurately
measure the distance
between the continents
and so monitor the precise
rate of plate movement.

FOSSIL EVIDENCE
Fossil remains of the long-extinct reptile
Lystrosaurus found in India, Africa, and
Antarctica provide the strongest evidence
that these separate continents were once
joined. Other fossils, such as those of the
Glossopteris fern, offer similar proof.

Eye
Nostril
Tooth

LYSTROSAURUS
SKULL

N. America
Europe
Asia
India
Australia
Pacific Ocean
Antarctica
S. America
Atlantic Ocean

3 Over the next 120 million years, the products of
this division became the continents, drifting closer
or further apart to take up their present positions.
The Americas emerged as separate continents, India
broke off from Africa and drifted towards Asia, and
Australia and Antarctica drifted south.

PLATE FACTS
• The west coast of
Africa perfectly mirrors
the east coast of South
America as they were
once joined together.

• Fossils of tropical
plants are found on the
Arctic island of
Spitsbergen because it
was once in the tropics.

Converging plates

In many places around the world, tectonic plates are slowly crunching together with enormous force. As they collide, one plate can be pushed underneath the other in a process called subduction. The plate is destroyed as it slides down into the heat of the Earth's mantle. Where the plates meet, deep trenches open up in the ocean floor.

THE *TRIESTE'S* DEEP DIVE
The Mariana Trench, the world's deepest, plunges to 10,863 m (35,640 ft). The bathyscape *Trieste* reached its floor, on 23 January 1960.

CONVERGENCE ZONES
This illustration shows where the Philippine plate and the Pacific Ocean plate push up against the Asian plate off the coast of Japan. The Philippines plate is subducted beneath the Asian plate, while the Pacific plate is subducted beneath both.

Japan

Hot blobs of magma burn their way through the overlying plate and erupt as volcanoes

Asian plate

Ocean trench

Ocean bed sediments scraped off to form a bank called an accretionary wedge

Philippines plate

Subducted plate melts as it descends into mantle

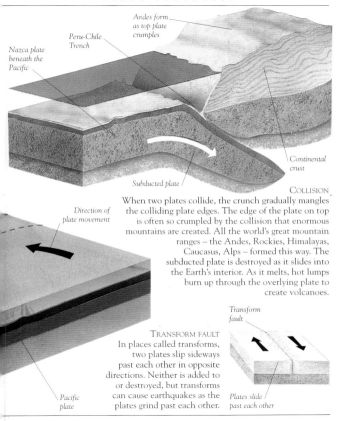

Andes form
as top plate
crumples

Peru-Chile
Trench

Nazca plate
beneath the
Pacific

Continental
crust

Subducted plate

Direction of
plate movement

Pacific
plate

COLLISION
When two plates collide, the crunch gradually mangles
the colliding plate edges. The edge of the plate on top
is often so crumpled by the collision that enormous
mountains are created. All the world's great mountain
ranges – the Andes, Rockies, Himalayas,
Caucasus, Alps – formed this way. The
subducted plate is destroyed as it slides into
the Earth's interior. As it melts, hot lumps
burn up through the overlying plate to
create volcanoes.

Transform
fault

TRANSFORM FAULT
In places called transforms,
two plates slip sideways
past each other in opposite
directions. Neither is added to
or destroyed, but transforms
can cause earthquakes as the
plates grind past each other.

Plates slide
past each other

Diverging plates

In many places along the ocean floor, tectonic plates are steadily moving further apart. As they do, molten rock from the Earth's interior wells up into the gap. When it meets the cold ocean water, the molten rock freezes to the edges of the plates, creating a series of jagged ridges along the ocean floor called a mid-ocean ridge.

MAPPING THE OCEAN
Oceanographers use echo-sounding, which bounces signals off the ocean floor, to map its contours.

THE WIDENING OCEANS
As plates pull apart, or diverge, the mid-ocean ridge gets wider as new rock is constantly added, and so the ocean floor spreads gradually wider. The widening floor of the Atlantic Ocean for example, is driving the Americas further away from Europe and Africa. The Mid-Atlantic ridge can be observed in Iceland, where it rises above the ocean surface.

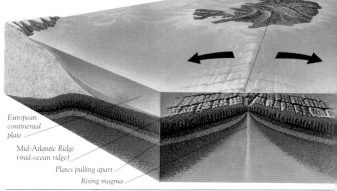

Median valley between two diverging plates

Iceland

European continental plate

Mid-Atlantic Ridge (mid-ocean ridge)

Plates pulling apart

Rising magma

SEA-FLOOR SPREADING

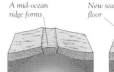

A mid-ocean ridge forms

New sea floor

Magma rises through cracks

Rock subsides
Fresh cracks in ridge

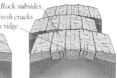

1 As the plates move apart, hot magma wells up from the mantle, emerging as lava. As the lava meets the cold sea water, it solidifies, freezing onto the edges of the plates.

2 As the old plate edges move further apart, the solidifying lava fills in the gap, forming new sea floor (oceanic crust). This is then pushed apart by magma rising from below.

3 When the tip of new rock gets too big, it snaps off under its own weight, subsiding into the mantle. The result is a series of scarp faces across the ridge wherever the tip cracks off.

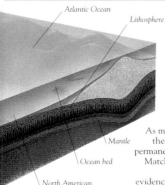

Atlantic Ocean

Lithosphere

Matching magnetic polarities

Magnetic "stripes" of rock

Magma

Mantle

Ocean bed

North American continental plate

MAGNETIC EVIDENCE
As molten rock solidifies, its particles align with the Earth's shifting magnetic field, providing a permanent record of the field's polarity at the time. Matching magnetic alignments in stripes of rock on either side of a mid-ocean ridge provide evidence of sea-floor spreading, indicating that the stripes must have been formed at the same time.

FAULTS

THE SLOW, UNSTOPPABLE movement of tectonic plates puts rocks under such enormous stress that they can twist and suddenly crack altogether. Where cracks, or "faults", appear, huge blocks of rock slip past each other, creating new cliffs, mountains, and valleys.

TRANSCURRENT FAULT

Where tectonic plates move sideways past one another at transform faults, wrench faults, also called strike-slip faults, often occur (see p. 21). The biggest wrench faults are called transcurrent faults. The famous San Andreas Fault in California, USA, was created by the Pacific plate grinding past the North American plate.

FAULT FACTS

• The Great Eastern African Rift Valley is over 3,000 km (1,864 miles) long.

• Land around the San Andreas fault moved over 6 m (20 ft) in the 1906 quake.

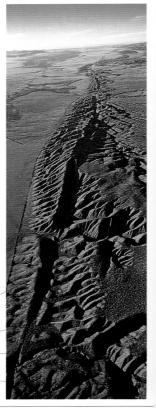

Stream diverted to follow fault line

North American plate moving southeast

Fault line

Pacific plate moving northwest

SAN ANDREAS FAULT

TYPES OF FAULT

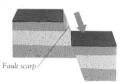

NORMAL FAULT
At a normal fault, blocks of rock move up or down, sometimes creating a huge cliff called a fault scarp.

Fault scarp

RIFT VALLEY
A long narrow block may sink between two parallel normal faults, forming a trough-shaped dip called a rift valley.

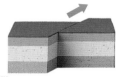

WRENCH FAULT
In a wrench, or strike-slip, fault, the rocks shear sideways and the blocks move horizontally past each other.

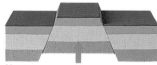

HORST
A horst is a block of rock thrown up between normal faults, that often creates vast plateaus or mountain ranges.

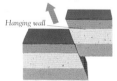

Hanging wall

REVERSE FAULT
In a reverse fault, one block is forced up over another, creating a fragile overhang called a hanging wall.

COMPLEX FAULTS
In complex fracture zones, a series of normal and reverse faults may tilt the blocks of rock in many directions.

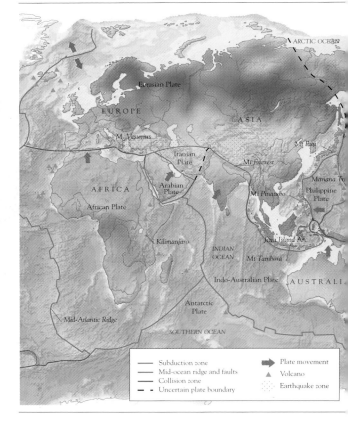

Subduction zone
Mid-ocean ridge and faults
Collision zone
Uncertain plate boundary

Plate movement
Volcano
Earthquake zone

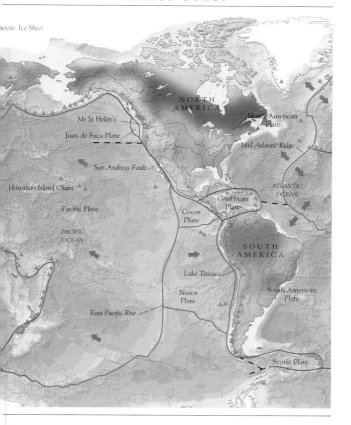

Arctic Ice Sheet

NORTH
AMERICA

North American
Plate

Mt St Helen's

Juan de Fuca Plate

Mid-Atlantic Ridge

San Andreas Fault

ATLANTIC
OCEAN

Hawaiian Island Chain

Caribbean
Plate

Pacific Plate

Cocos
Plate

PACIFIC
OCEAN

SOUTH
AMERICA

Lake Titicaca

Nazca
Plate

South American
Plate

East Pacific Rise

Scotia Plate

Where disaster may strike

A volcano can have a lifespan of a million years or more, and centuries can pass between eruptions. So, it is not always easy to identify which volcanoes are dangerous, or 'active' – likely to erupt at any time – and which are 'dormant', or sleeping, or 'extinct', and never likely to erupt again. This is why the official list of active volcanoes compiled by the Smithsonian Institute, in Washington, USA, lists those that have erupted in the last 10,000 years – a total of over 1,500 world wide.

THE RING OF FIRE
Many of the world's most violent and active volcanoes occur in a ring around the Pacific Ocean, known as the "Ring of Fire". They include Pinatubo in the Philippines and Fujiyama in Japan.

San Andreas Fault, California

Carribean Plate

Philippine Plate

Great Barrier Reef

Tonga trench

Mount Cook, New Zealand

Aconcagua, Chile, the world's tallest volcano

There are 75 strato-volcanoes in Chile, while Indonesia has more than 80

STRATOVOLCANOES
The most explosive volcanoes occur in the places where tectonic plates collide, usually subduction zones. The forced blending of plate material creates the sticky rhyolitic and dacitic (see pp. 36–37) magma that encourages sudden, violent eruptions and leaves steep, cone-shaped stratovolcanoes.

SHIELD VOLCANOES

The crust under the ocean is thin, so lava here is basaltic, uncontaminated by other rocks, and very runny. So volcanoes over ocean hot spots are shield volcanoes, which gush steadily.

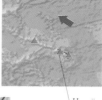

Hawaiian hot spots

VOLCANO FACTS
• Worldwide, there are 1,511 known volcanoes.
• 500 active volcanoes result in 60 major eruptions a year.
• In the last 10,000 years, only four of these were as explosive as the 1815 Tambora eruption.

RIFT VOLCANOES

Where hot spots occur in the middle of continents, the magma is contaminated by continental crustal materials. Such volcanoes may not be as active or as explosive as those near subduction zones, but can still build up into huge cone-shaped peaks such as Mount Kilimanjaro in Tanzania, and Yellowstone, USA, with successive eruptions.

MID-OCEAN RIDGES

Volcanoes erupt along mid-ocean ridges where tectonic plates pull apart. Thousands of volcanoes form here, most of which are quietly erupting fissure volcanoes or hydrothermal vents. Their activity is deep beneath the ocean.

Iceland

Mid-ocean ridge

Hot-spot volcanoes rear spectacularly above the ocean surface

Mendocino Fracture Zone

San Andreas, a transform fault, produces shallow but destructive quakes

DEEP QUAKE

Ninety per cent of deep quakes and 75 per cent of mid-level quakes occur around the Pacific. Most of the rest occur in the Alpine-Himalayan belt. Transform faults create smaller, shallower quakes, but these send out mostly damaging surface waves.

VOLCANIC ERUPTIONS

FIRE FROM BELOW

DESPITE THE HEAT of the Earth's interior, great pressure keeps most rock in the mantle solid. So, how is the liquid magma that supplies volcanoes created? Mantle rock melts into floods of magma, and collects along plate margins. Buoyed by its light weight, it then wells to the surface to erupt as volcanoes.

MELT NETWORKS
Even though it is solid, mantle rock can creep upwards. As it nears the surface, and the pressure drops, the rock can expand and start to melt. Melting begins on the edge of crystal grains in the rock, and quickly makes a linked network of microscopic tubes through which huge quantities of liquid magma can ooze towards the surface, like oil squeezed from a sponge.

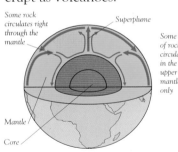

Some rock circulates right through the mantle

Superplume

Some currents of rock circulate in the upper mantle only

Mantle

Core

CURRENTS IN THE MANTLE
The mantle churns slowly, as hot material rises to the surface, then cools and sinks, creating circular convection currents. If a slab of subducted plate sinks through the mantle to the core, a hot blob or "superplume" rises, forcing magma to the surface.

VOLCANIC ERUPTIONS
Mantle rock brought to the surface by circulating currents may make magma available for volcanic eruptions.

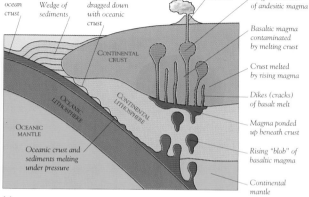

Basaltic ocean crust

Wedge of sediments

Sediments dragged down with oceanic crust

Volcano

Magma chamber of andesitic magma

Basaltic magma contaminated by melting crust

CONTINENTAL CRUST

Crust melted by rising magma

OCEANIC LITHOSPHERE

CONTINENTAL LITHOSPHERE

Dikes (cracks) of basalt melt

OCEANIC MANTLE

Magma ponded up beneath crust

Oceanic crust and sediments melting under pressure

Rising "blob" of basaltic magma

Continental mantle

MIXED MAGMA

The materials that melt in mantle rock usually form basaltic magma, which is light and floats up towards the surface. Where the melt forms from a subducted plate, blobs of basalt magma rise up against the underside of the continental crust. Since the magma is so hot, it melts its way through. Silica, sodium, and potassium in crystal rocks are partially melted by the magma and mix in with it. This makes the magma more acidic and viscous, increasing the chance of explosive eruptions.

MAGMA LAYERS

Laboratory experiments have shown that this "mixed" magma may crystallize in layers of different minerals, for example, olivine, and pyroxene.

MAGMA FACTS

• A superplume may have caused the flood basalt eruptions during the Cretaceous period, 100 million years ago.

• Basalt magma can reach temperatures of up to 1,200°C (2,192°F).

Peridot is the gem variety of the mineral olivine

VOLCANIC ERUPTIONS

VOLCANOES ERUPT because the hot magma (liquid rock) in the Earth's interior is less dense than the overlying solid rock. Wherever there is a crack in the rock, magma rises up and oozes through onto the surface. Where there is no crack, pressure may build up until the magma bursts out.

Nearer the surface, various gases form ever larger bubbles

Bubbles continue to expand as magma rises up and pressure falls

Tiny bubbles form in magma as it rises through the chamber

GAS POWER
Magma can be driven from the ground by the carbon dioxide and steam in it. As it nears the surface, bubbles of gas propel the molten rock from the vent.

ERUPTION FACTS
• At 36 m (120 ft) below ground, pressure is ten times as high as it is on the surface.
• Gas expands ten times in volume as it rises from 36 m (120 ft) down to the surface.

REPEAT ERUPTIONS
Volcanoes usually erupt again and again. The repose time – the time between eruptions – can vary from a few minutes to thousands of years, and occasionally displays a distinct rhythm. Hawaii's Kilauea volcano erupts once a month, but most volcanoes are less regular.

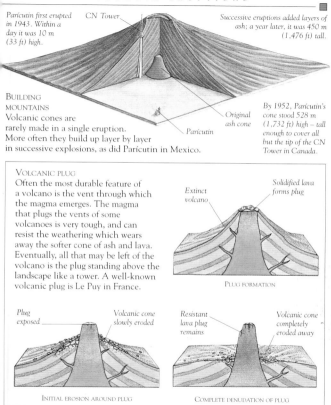

Parícutin first erupted in 1943. Within a day it was 10 m (33 ft) high.

CN Tower

Successive eruptions added layers of ash; a year later, it was 450 m (1,476 ft) tall.

BUILDING MOUNTAINS

Volcanic cones are rarely made in a single eruption. More often they build up layer by layer in successive explosions, as did Parícutin in Mexico.

Original ash cone

Parícutin

By 1952, Parícutin's cone stood 528 m (1,732 ft) high – tall enough to cover all but the tip of the CN Tower in Canada.

VOLCANIC PLUG

Often the most durable feature of a volcano is the vent through which the magma emerges. The magma that plugs the vents of some volcanoes is very tough, and can resist the weathering which wears away the softer cone of ash and lava. Eventually, all that may be left of the volcano is the plug standing above the landscape like a tower. A well-known volcanic plug is Le Puy in France.

Extinct volcano

Solidified lava forms plug

PLUG FORMATION

Plug exposed

Volcanic cone slowly eroded

Resistant lava plug remains

Volcanic cone completely eroded away

INITIAL EROSION AROUND PLUG

COMPLETE DENUDATION OF PLUG

Types of eruption

No volcano is quite the same. Each has its own particular shape and way of erupting – and each eruption is slightly different. Volcanoes can be classified into several different groups according to the way they erupt. A groups is usually named after a classic eruption of its type.

Steam billows from shallow sea volcano

SUBMARINE

Steam makes eruptions much more powerful, as it can explode with over a third as much energy as TNT. During a submarine eruption in shallow seas – less than 300 m (900 ft) deep – water in the volcano's vent can explode violently.

Plateaus of lava spread far from fissure

FISSURE

In a fissure eruption, floods of hot, runny lava pour from a crack in the ground: this can be many kilometres long. As the lava reaches the surface, a fall in pressure allows the gases it holds to boil suddenly, shooting fountains of lava into the air.

Runny lava from single vent

Fire fountains shoot into the sky

Sporadic eruptions blast ash and hot lava into air

Steep cone formed by sticky lava which does not flow far

HAWAIIAN

Like fissures, Hawaiian eruptions gush lava and fire, but the lava pours from a single vent rather than a crack, creating a dome-shaped mountain. These are known as shield volcanoes, because they are shaped like shields.

STROMBOLIAN

In eruptions where magma is sticky, gases escape eratically, and volcanoes spit out sizzling clots of lava sporadically. These eruptions, which form a steep cone, are named after Stromboli, an active volcano on an island off southwest Italy.

Explosive bursts eject ash clouds into the air

Alternating layers of ash and lava build up steep cone, known as stratovolcano or composite cone

Ash clouds as high as 18 km (11 miles) affect climate and cause dramatic sunsets

VULCANIAN

A Vulcanian volcano is very explosive and unpredictable. In vulcanian eruptions, magma is so sticky that the vent clogs up between cannon-like blasts that eject ash clouds and fragments of magma, followed by thick lava flows.

Burning clouds of ash and gas consume everything in their way

Ash and lava shoot out of vent like bullets until magma chamber is almost empty

PELEAN

Named after Mount Pelée in Martinique, Pelean eruptions feature glowing clouds of ash and gas, called *nuée ardentes*, that roar down the mountain at tremendous speeds. With stratovolcanoes, the ash forms a skirt around the foot of the cone.

PLINIAN

The most explosive of all are Plinian eruptions, named after Pliny the Younger, who witnessed the eruption of Vesuvius in AD 79. Boiling gases blast clouds of ash and volcanic fragments into the stratosphere.

EXPLOSIVE VOLCANOES

VOLCANOES CAN EXPLODE when viscous magma, rich in gas and steam, clogs the volcano's vent, so pressure builds up until the magma bursts through. The release in pressure lets the steam boil, blasting magma, hot ash, gas, and steam into the air.

Mount Cotopaxi

ANDESITE VOLCANOES

The cooler magma is and the richer it is in silica, the stickier it is. The stickiest magmas are in subduction zones. Such magmas are called andesitic, after the Andes in South America, where Mount Cotopaxi is the highest volcano.

FORMATION OF A CALDERA

Magma chamber

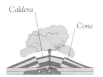

Caldera

Cone

Lake

1 In an active volcano, the magma chamber beneath the cone is full of molten magma that has risen up from the mantle.

2 If the level of magma in the chamber beneath the volcano drops, the top of the cone may collapse into it, forming a giant crater called a caldera.

3 When the volcano begins to die down, the rest of the cone collapses and the caldera may fill with water to form a crater lake.

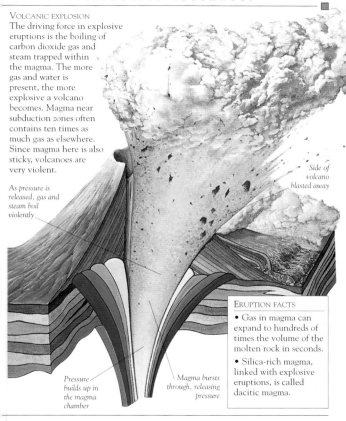

VOLCANIC EXPLOSION
The driving force in explosive eruptions is the boiling of carbon dioxide gas and steam trapped within the magma. The more gas and water is present, the more explosive a volcano becomes. Magma near subduction zones often contains ten times as much gas as elsewhere. Since magma here is also sticky, volcanoes are very violent.

As pressure is released, gas and steam boil violently

Side of volcano blasted away

Pressure builds up in the magma chamber

Magma bursts through, releasing pressure

ERUPTION FACTS
• Gas in magma can expand to hundreds of times the volume of the molten rock in seconds.

• Silica-rich magma, linked with explosive eruptions, is called dacitic magma.

LAVA

MAGMA THAT HAS erupted onto the surface is called lava. The lava from explosive volcanoes is thick and pasty and spreads in thick, slow-moving flows. These can be hundreds of metres deep but rarely reach more than a few kilometres from the vent.

WAXY OR LUMPY
Runny lava cools and solidifies into smooth lobes that look like huge blobs of black candle wax. Pasty lava looks more lumpy.

CREEPING LAVA
Runny lava flows in rivers of red-hot molten rock, but pasty lava creeps forward just a few metres a day. The surface continually cools to a thick skin, which breaks every now and then as the red-hot lava oozes forward underneath. Big blocks ride on top of the flow and occasionally avalanche down its steep front wall, sending up clouds of dust. Lava flows like this are so slow moving that they are rarely dangerous – but they are almost impossible to stop.

DACITE   RHYOLITE

Obsidian is coloured by minerals

TYPES OF LAVA
There are four main types of lava –
basalt, andesite, dacite, and rhyolite.
Basaltic lava has a silica content of about
50 per cent and, when molten, is as
runny as honey. Andesite is 55 per cent
silica and as sticky as treacle. Dacitic
lava is 65 per cent silica and has the
consistency of hot tar. Rhyolite is 73 per
cent silica and is more like cold tar.

GLASSY LAVA
If lava cools very rapidly – in minutes
rather than days or years – there is no
time for crystals to grow. It hardens
into a smooth rock such as shiny black
obsidian, which, like window glass,
is made up mainly of silicon dioxide.

Lichens – the first signs of life on lava

PUMICE

FROTHY LAVA
Some lava is so frothy with bubbles that
when it cools and solidifies it is as full of
tiny holes as a sponge. This frothy
volcanic rock is called pumice, and it
is so light that it actually floats in water.
Pumice can be used for scouring skin.

LIFE FROM LAVA
Volcanic ash is rich in minerals and
makes fertile soil. Lava itself, however,
makes a hostile environment and it may
be many years before the first lichens
can be seen. Eventually mosses, grasses,
shrubs, and trees will take a hold.

VOLCANIC DEBRIS

WHEN AN EXPLOSIVE volcano erupts, large lumps of volcanic material are hurled into the air. Pyroclasts (meaning "fire-broken") or blocks, are shattered chunks of volcanic rock, blown apart by the explosion. Volcanic bombs are blobs of molten magma that cool and harden in flight.

Red-hot tephra

Cinder

Volcanic bomb

Volcanic block

Lapilli

VOLCANIC BLITZ

Pyroclasts and bombs blasted high into the air during an eruption are called tephra. Major eruptions can shoot chunks of tephra weighing a tonne or more 1,500 m (1 mile) upwards at the speed of a jet plane. Most chunks land near the vent, but if they are ejected at the right angle some may be hurled several kilometres away.

BOMBS

Volcanic bombs are red-hot and soft, and as they hurtle through the air they can be twisted into all kinds of shapes. "Breadcrust" bombs, for example, stretch into a loaf shape, with the "crust" cracked by the expanding gases inside.

BLOCKS

Most volcanic blocks are fragments of the old volcanic plug, which is blasted from the vent as the volcano erupts. Blocks are generally much more angular in shape than bombs. They are typically 0.3–1 m (12–40 in) in diameter.

CINDERS AND LAPILLI

Smaller pyroclasts are called cinders or lapilli, depending on their size. Cinders are rough lumps 6.4–30 cm (2.5–12 in) in diameter. Lapilli, (which means "little stone"), are smaller, nut-size lumps that measure 0.2–6.4 cm (0.1–2.5 in) across.

PELE'S HAIR

When hot, runny lava is ejected from a volcano, small drops may be drawn out into long, light, glassy threads as they fly through the air. These spiky, hair-like strands can be up to 1 m (3 ft) long and are often blown several kilometres before landing. These threads are called Pele's hair, after Pele, the Hawaiian goddess of volcanoes.

Fine, needle-like strands

DEBRIS FACTS

• With explosive volcanoes, 90 per cent of ejected material is in the form of pyroclasts and volcanic ash.

ASH AND DUST

WHEN THEY ERUPT, explosive volcanoes can blast old volcanic rock into tiny pieces, and hurl huge quantities of dust, ash, and cinders into the air. Ash clouds can billow more than a dozen kilometres up and then fall like snow far around the volcano, covering hills, valleys and villages with a choking grey layer.

Pyroclastic flow deposit

Pyroclastic surge deposits

Ash and lapilli

Temperatures can reach 800°C (1,472°F)

The mix of ash and expanding gas makes a nuée ardente flow like a fluid

TELL-TALE LAYERS
Volcanic deposits from the Vesuvius eruption of AD 79 (pp. 50–53) clearly reveal the sequence of events. The town of Pompeii was buried by 2 m (6 ft) of ash and lapilli, followed by two pyroclastic flows and a large surge.

PYROCLASTIC FLOW
In some eruptions, ash and pyroclasts are not thrown up in the air, but are blasted sideways or fall back down onto the side of the volcano, forming scorching avalanches called pyroclastic flows, or *nuée ardentes* (glowing clouds). These can move at up to 500 km/h (300 mph), incinerating everything in their path.

ASH
Volcanic ash is made up of particles less than 2 mm (0.1 in) in diameter. Ash is ejected in huge quantities – the 1912 eruption of Mount Katmai in Alaska, USA, for example, ejected 20 cu km (4.8 cu miles) of ashfall.

DUST
Volcanic dust is a mix of tiny glass and mineral particles. It is lighter than ash and takes longer to fall to the ground. Dust can be blasted high into the stratosphere, lingering in the air for months, or even years.

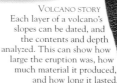

Ash layers

TUFF
Thick ashfalls and pyroclastic flow deposits are eventually washed away by rain, or harden where they lay. When they harden, the volcanic material is compacted, forming a rock called tuff.

VOLCANO STORY
Each layer of a volcano's slopes can be dated, and the contents and depth analyzed. This can show how large the eruption was, how much material it produced, and how long it lasted.

EFFUSIVE VOLCANOES

MANY VOLCANOES do not explode violently, but ooze lava almost continuously. These effusive, or flowing, volcanoes occur where the magma is fairly runny and low in gas. In basaltic magma like this, the gases have time to leak out before it reaches the surface. So the lava sprays out of the ground in a fountain of fire, or wells out as a stream of molten rock.

When pahoehoe reaches the sea, it sizzles gently into the water

PAHOEHOE LAVA

Effusive volcanoes produce two types of lava, known by their Hawaiian names of pahoehoe and aa. Pahoehoe is hot, runny lava that flows freely. As its surface cools, it forms a wrinkled, rope-like skin. Pahoehoe typically oozes forward in shallow, tongue-like flows, moving at about 1 m (3 ft) a minute.

AA LAVA

When lava fountains spray molten rock into the air, it cools and clots as it falls. This creates a crumbly, lumpy lava called aa. Aa shuffles forward in surges, falling over itself like a bulldozer track.

Lithosphere

LAVA GUSHERS

Effusive volcanoes produce a lot of lava and hardly any ash or cinders. The lava floods out far across the landscape in broad flows – sometimes hundreds of kilometres across. Volcanoes like this rarely form steep-sided cones. Instead they form shallow plateaus and are called shield volcanoes.

BASALT LAVA FACTS

• Basaltic lava is less than 50 per cent silica.

• At over 1,200°C (2,192°F), basalt lava is much hotter than both andesitic (1,000°C/1,832°F) and dacitic (800°C/1,472°F) lavas.

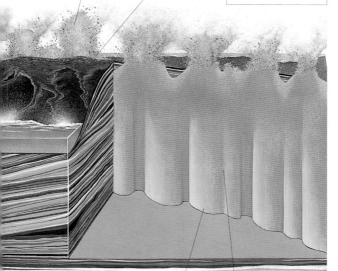

When aa hits the ocean it can cause steam explosions.

Fire fountains of lava spray from surface fissures

Dark, runny basaltic lava quickly floods out across the landscape

Magma begins to rise through the lithosphere 60 km (37 miles) below the Earth's surface

Magma wells up through huge curtain-like cracks in the ground

BLACK SMOKERS

TALL CHIMNEYS BELCHING clouds of hot black smoke exist down on the sea floor. Research into these intriguing volcanic features has revealed that they support organisms that live at very high temperatures.

HYDROTHERMAL VENTS

Black smokers, or hydrothermal vents, form along mid-ocean ridges where tectonic plates are moving apart. Sea water seeping through cracks in the sea floor is heated by the magma and dissolves minerals from the rock. As it is heated, the water spews from vents in scalding mineral-rich plumes. Rapid cooling leaves deposits of sulphur, iron, zinc, and copper in tall chimneys.

Riftia, giant tube worms, live off bacteria inside their bodies

MANGANESE NODULES
Slow-forming nodules of manganese deposited by black smokers carpet the Pacific floor. These minerals may be harvested industrially in the future.

LIVING OFF CHEMICALS

Black smokers are home to a community of organisms that thrive in the scalding waters and toxic chemicals that would be lethal to other creatures. Elsewhere, life depends ultimately on green plants absorbing sunlight; here, organisms depend on the bacteria which feed on the chemicals, especially hydrogen sulphide.

Giant clams thrive on bacteria inside their bodies

Eelpouts feed on tube worms

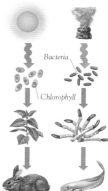

Bacteria

Chlorophyll

Surface plants use chlorophyll to turn sunlight into basic food, and are then in turn eaten by animals.

In the ocean depths, bacteria in tube worms and other simple organisms turn sulphur in the water into food.

BLACK SMOKER FACTS

• Vents can be up to 50 m (165 ft) tall.

• Each drop of sea water circulates through vents every ten million years.

• Water jetting from black smokers can reach 662°C (1,224°F).

VOLCANIC ISLANDS

SOME VOLCANOES ERUPT far from plate margins.
These hot-spot volcanoes occur where rising columns
of hot magma in the mantle, called mantle plumes,
burn their way straight through the plate. The thin
plates at the bottom of the ocean are most easily
pierced by hot spots. Where the volcanoes rise
above the ocean surface they form islands.

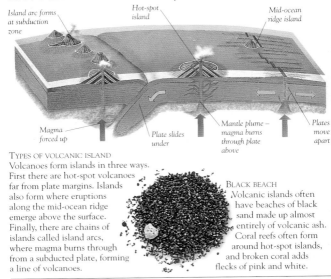

Island arc forms
at subduction
zone

Hot-spot
island

Mid-ocean
ridge island

Magma
forced up

Plate slides
under

Mantle plume –
magma burns
through plate
above

Plates
move
apart

TYPES OF VOLCANIC ISLAND
Volcanoes form islands in three ways.
First there are hot-spot volcanoes
far from plate margins. Islands
also form where eruptions
along the mid-ocean ridge
emerge above the surface.
Finally, there are chains of
islands called island arcs,
where magma burns through
from a subducted plate, forming
a line of volcanoes.

BLACK BEACH
Volcanic islands often
have beaches of black
sand made up almost
entirely of volcanic ash.
Coral reefs often form
around hot-spot islands,
and broken coral adds
flecks of pink and white.

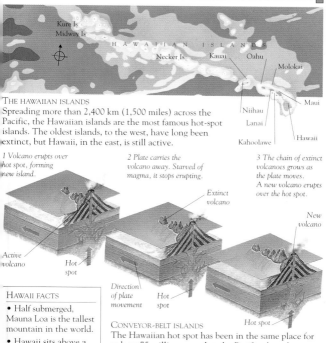

THE HAWAIIAN ISLANDS

Spreading more than 2,400 km (1,500 miles) across the Pacific, the Hawaiian islands are the most famous hot-spot islands. The oldest islands, to the west, have long been extinct, but Hawaii, in the east, is still active.

1 Volcano erupts over hot spot, forming new island.

2 Plate carries the volcano away. Starved of magma, it stops erupting.

3 The chain of extinct volcanoes grows as the plate moves. A new volcano erupts over the hot spot.

Extinct volcano

Active volcano

Hot spot

Direction of plate movement

Hot spot

New volcano

Hot spot

HAWAII FACTS

• Half submerged, Mauna Loa is the tallest mountain in the world.

• Hawaii sits above a pool of magma 300 km (200 miles) wide.

• The island of Hawaii keeps growing in size.

CONVEYOR-BELT ISLANDS

The Hawaiian hot spot has been in the same place for at least 75 million years, but the Pacific plate above it is moving at a rate of 10 cm (4 in) a year. As magma burns through the plate above, a new volcano is created over the hot spot. Each one dies out as the plate moves away from the hot spot, but before long, another volcano emerges over the pool of magma.

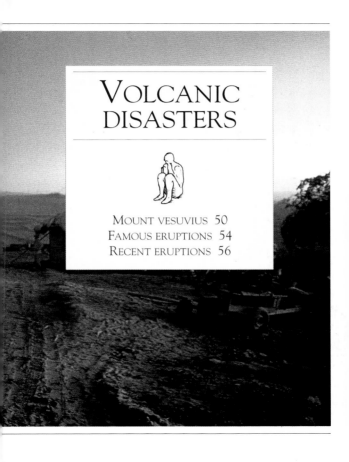

VOLCANIC DISASTERS

MOUNT VESUVIUS

ONE OF THE most famous eruptions in history took place on 24 August AD 79, when Italy's Mount Vesuvius buried the Roman town of Pompeii in vast quantities of hot ash. The remains of Pompeii were discovered in the 18th century, almost perfectly preserved under several metres of ash, providing a snapshot of ancient Roman life.

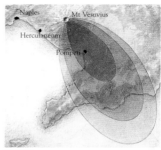

ILL WIND
When Vesuvius erupted, a northwest wind blew the vast cloud of ash straight towards the thriving town of Pompeii, where for two days it fell like snow.

VESUVIUS FACTS

- The explosion blew away the entire top of the mountain.
- Up to 10 cm (4 in) of ash fell 100 km (60 miles) from Pompeii.
- Before that day, Vesuvius had lain dormant for 800 years; since then, it has erupted several times.

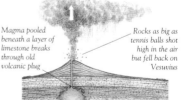

Magma pooled beneath a layer of limestone breaks through old volcanic plug

Rocks as big as tennis balls shot high in the air but fell back on Vesuvius

THE ERUPTION

1 Magma sitting in an underground chamber over 10 km (6 miles) wide burst through a plug of volcanic material in Vesuvius' vent, shooting a vast cloud of pumice and ash high into the air.

ENTOMBED CITY
Ash buried Pompeii to a depth of 6–7 m (19–23 ft). When rain fell the next day, the ash set like concrete, preserving the town exactly as it was when the mountain blew. Pompeii was abandoned and local people forgot both its location and name, calling it "the City". When archaeologists began to dig, Pompeii's remarkable wall paintings and numerous other details of Roman life were revealed.

Both murals and graffiti have been found on Pompeii's walls. One girl, Livia, wrote to Alexander, "Do you think I would mind if you dropped dead tomorrow?"

Dining tables were preserved with half-eaten meals still on them.

In an attempt to escape from the choking ash people used cloths to filter the hot ash-laden air

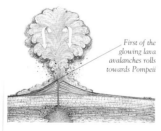

First of the glowing lava avalanches rolls towards Pompeii

2 A huge cloud of finer material spread far and wide, blotting out the sun, before slowly burying vast areas in debris. Larger fragments fell back into the hot gases and lava spewing from the volcano.

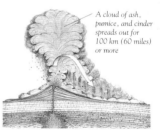

A cloud of ash, pumice, and cinder spreads out for 100 km (60 miles) or more

3 A deadly swirl of gases and volcanic fragments roared down the slope towards Pompeii. Already overcome by ash, its inhabitants had no chance of surviving this pyroclastic surge.

Pompeii – the lost city

When Vesuvius erupted and engulfed Pompeii, the tragedy left two remarkable legacies: the astonishing remains of both Pompeii and nearby Herculaneum, and an eyewitness account of the eruption written by Pliny the Younger. He was staying across the Bay of Naples with his uncle, the Roman scholar Pliny the Elder, who died from the gases.

VICTIM OF THE
BLAST "FROZEN"
IN TIME

FRESH FIG

CARBONIZED FOOD
Food normally burns away in intense heat, but at Pompeii carbon dioxide in the hot gases turned the food to charcoal, so preserving the half-eaten meals of the inhabitants for 2,000 years.

BOWL OF CARBONIZED FIGS

POMPEII FACTS

• Herculaneum was covered with five times more debris than Pompeii.

• Most victims died from suffocation.

VICTIMS
OF VESUVIUS
More than 2,000 people died at Pompeii, their bodies encased in ash that set like cement around them. The corpses rotted away, leaving just bones, but the hollow impressions of the bodies showed how the unfortunate victims were caught – cowering, running, or clinging together.

CAST OF SUFFOCATED BABY,
FOUND IN A PLACE NOW NAMED
THE GARDEN OF THE FUGITIVES

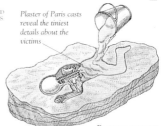

*Plaster of Paris casts
reveal the tiniest
details about the
victims*

PLASTER CASTER
When archaeologist Giuseppe Fiorelli
began working on the Pompeii site in
1860, he devised a very effective way of
preserving the hollows left by the victim's
bodies. Whenever a hollow was discovered,
he quickly filled it with wet plaster of Paris.
After the plaster hardened, the cast could
safely be dug out and preserved.

HERCULANEUM
When Vesuvius erupted, the Roman
seaside resort of Herculaneum escaped
the ashfall – but was devastated by a
sudden avalanche of glowing hot ash
and mud. When at first archaeologists
found very few bodies in the town, it
was assumed that the inhabitants
must have had enough warning to
flee to safety. Then, in the 1980s,
hundreds of skeletons were found
beneath the massive brick arches
that once stood on the shore,
huddled together where they had
tried to escape the deadly blast.

FAMOUS ERUPTIONS

EVERY NOW AND THEN the tragic consequences of an eruption, or its sheer scale, leaves an indelible mark on history. The awesome explosion of Krakatoa in 1883 was heard a quarter of the way around the world, but a much smaller eruption on the Caribbean island of Martinique in 1903 had a far higher death toll.

Active cone at Barren Island, Sumatra, inside older volcanic crater

TAMBORA, INDONESIA

The hundreds of islands of Indonesia have seen some of the world's largest volcanic explosions. In 1815, one of the biggest recorded eruptions, on Tambora, ejected 80 cu km (59.5 cu miles) of ash, compared to 3 cu km (2.2 cu miles) at Vesuvius, killing 90,000 Indonesians.

PUMICE FROM KRAKATOA

KRAKATOA, WEST OF JAVA

Before it erupted in 1883, Krakatoa was an uninhabited island between Java and Sumatra. On 26 August, the island blew up with such a deafening roar that the eardrums of sailors over 40 km (25 miles) away were shattered, and it was heard in Alice Springs, Australia. Dust and gas coloured sunsets as far away as Europe, while the moon turned blue for months.

St Pierre, Martinique

The destruction of St Pierre

Despite their awesome power, volcanoes are rarely as deadly as earthquakes as there is often time for people to escape before their worst effects hit. But the inhabitants of St Pierre had no chance of escape when Mount Pelée erupted on 8 May 1902. All but two of the 29,000 townspeople were incinerated in minutes by the horrific pyroclastic flow that swept down the mountain and over the city.

Auguste Ciparis, a prisoner condemned to death, was one of only two people to survive the blast, protected by the thick walls of his cell.

Top of charred human femur (thigh bone) found in the destroyed city

Searing heat has distorted glass

GLASS BOTTLE FROM ST PIERRE

TIME STOPS
This pocket watch found in the ruins was melted to a stop less than 20 minutes after the eruption began.

RECENT ERUPTIONS

GEOLOGICAL EVIDENCE shows that some volcanic eruptions in the past were of cataclysmic size. No recent eruption has matched these prehistoric monsters, but even so, all eruptions are headline news today. Pictures are beamed rapidly around the world, and teams of vulcanologists flock to see what they can learn.

SURTSEY FACTS

- Within three years of forming, Surtsey was inhabited by plants, insects, and birds.
- Surtsey formed where the plates of the Mid-Atlantic Ridge part.

SURTSEY

One of the most remarkable volcanic events of recent years was the appearance of a new volcanic island, that rose from the waves off Iceland almost overnight. It began on 15 November 1963, when fishermen rushed towards a cloud of dark smoke on the horizon, thinking it was a boat on fire. Within ten days, the new island of Surtsey was 900 m (3,000 ft) long and 650 m (2,165 ft) wide. It formed in a sea over 130 m (435 ft) deep.

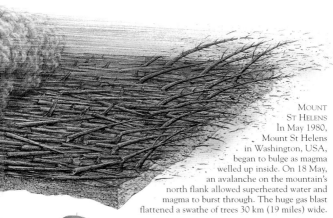

MOUNT
ST HELENS
In May 1980,
Mount St Helens
in Washington, USA,
began to bulge as magma
welled up inside. On 18 May,
an avalanche on the mountain's
north flank allowed superheated water and
magma to burst through. The huge gas blast
flattened a swathe of trees 30 km (19 miles) wide.

PINATUBO, THE PHILIPPINES
In April 1991, small
explosions on Mount
Pinatubo warned of an
imminent eruption. When
the volcano blew in June
that year, 100,000 people
had been safely evacuated.

MONTSERRAT
Just how vulnerable life in
the shadow of a volcano
can be became clear on
the Caribbean island of
Montserrat in June 1997.
Regarded as a tropical
paradise by both its
inhabitants and visitors,
little thought was given to
the long dormant volcano
until it destroyed the
capital city of Plymouth,
and so devastating the
island's fragile economy.

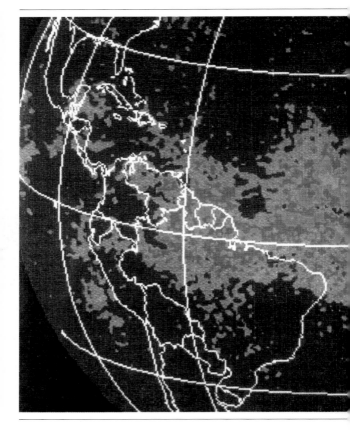

VOLCANOES AND THE ENVIRONMENT

VOLCANIC INTRUSIONS

NOT ALL VOLCANIC activity takes place on the surface. Magma bubbling up through the crust is often trapped underground. As it pushes into overlying rock, it forms igneous intrusions, by filling in gaps in existing rock structures – concordant intrusions – or by cracking and breaking through surrounding rock – discordant intrusions.

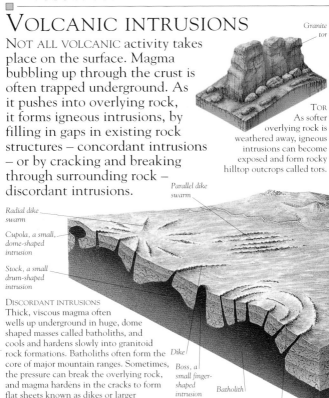

Granite tor

TOR
As softer overlying rock is weathered away, igneous intrusions can become exposed and form rocky hilltop outcrops called tors.

Parallel dike swarm

Radial dike swarm

Cupola, a small, dome-shaped intrusion

Stock, a small drum-shaped intrusion

DISCORDANT INTRUSIONS
Thick, viscous magma often wells up underground in huge, dome shaped masses called batholiths, and cools and hardens slowly into granitoid rock formations. Batholiths often form the core of major mountain ranges. Sometimes, the pressure can break the overlying rock, and magma hardens in the cracks to form flat sheets known as dikes or larger intrusions – stocks, bosses, and cupolas.

Dike

Boss, a small finger-shaped intrusion

Batholith

Ring dikes

Resistant hard rock that is slow to erode

Softer rock undercut by other rocks and water

WATERFALL

Igneous intrusions, often harder than the surrounding "country" rock, may eventually be exposed as country rock wears away. When a river flows over a sill, a waterfall may form where it wears away the soft rock beneath.

Granite tor

Granite half-dome

Cedar-tree laccolith, where laccoliths are stacked

Lopolith, a large lens-shaped intrusion

Phacolith, a small lens-shaped intrusion

CONCORDANT INTRUSIONS

Runny magma that cools into basalt-like rocks tends to mould itself into the country rock, following existing lines of weakness and bedding planes. Where it flows between layers, it hardens to form horizontal sheets called sills, such as Palisades Sill in New Jersey, USA, and Salisbury Crags in Scotland. Lens-shaped lopoliths and phacoliths form in downfolds in the rock, and laccoliths form where magma pushes up the layers in an upfold.

Sill

Laccolith, an up-arching intrusion

STEAM, MUD, AND GEYSERS

ROCK AND MAGMA under the ground stays hot long after a volcano has ceased erupting and the surface has cooled. Rain or snow trickling through the ground may be heated and bubble up to the surface to form hot springs, geysers and mud-pots, or mix with gases to form fumaroles and solfataras.

HOT SPRINGS
The Blue Pool in Iceland is filled with naturally hot water that has been heated underground and emerges in hot springs. Many people believe that these mineral-rich waters help to cure illness and aid relaxation.

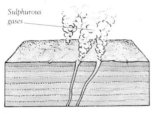

Sulphurous gases

SOLFATARAS
In places, steam created by heated water mixes with sulphurous fumes from magma to create solfataras. The ancient Romans believed their underworld lay beneath the volcano La Solfatara, near Pozzuoli, Italy, and the poet Virgil wrote of the wispy fumes as bodiless spirits.

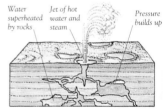

Water superheated by rocks

Jet of hot water and steam

Pressure builds up

GEYSERS
Water in deep underground conduits may be superheated at pressure to over 300°C (572°F) without boiling. As water closer to the surface boils, it releases the pressure and the superheated water flashes into steam and shoots upwards. Geysers spout every time the conduit fills with water.

CRYSTAL WATERFALLS

Hot water can dissolve minerals, which are then deposited when the water from hot springs emerges onto the surface and cools. These minerals, such as travertine, can form striking rings and waterfall-like features, such as the Pummukale deposits in Turkey (above).

TRAVERTINE

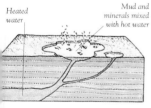

Heated water

Mud and minerals mixed with hot water

Superheated water

Steam

MUD-POTS

Where water lingers underground and easily dissolves rocks, hot water may become thick with minerals. As it oozes to the surface to form mud-pots, bubbles of mud burst at the surface with a strange flopping sound. Bathing in cooler mud-pots is thought to be good for the skin.

FUMAROLES

Fumaroles are vents that often occur on the side of volcanoes, and issue thick, often sulphurous, gas. While they were once thought to be linked to dormant or dying volcanoes, it is now clear that they may warn of imminent eruptions, as they did at Mount St Helens in 1980.

WEATHER AND CLIMATE

WHEN A BIG VOLCANO erupts, the effects on local weather can be dramatic. Dust clouds block the sun light, lightning flashes, updraughts set off violent winds, and condensing steam falls in torrents of rain. If dust blasts into the stratosphere, it can also affect weather world wide.

SCARLET SKIES
The vivid, atmospheric skies of the English artist J. M. W. Turner (1775–1851) may have been inspired by dust-filled sunsets following the eruption in Tambora, Indonesia, in 1815.

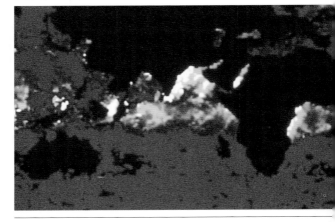

DINOSAUR DOOM
Many scientists think that the dinosaurs died out when dust clouds turned the world cold and dark. These could have resulted from a huge eruption or from the impact of a meteorite hitting Earth.

THE SUNLESS YEAR
Dust thrown up by the eruption in Tambora may have cut down sunlight around the world. In 1816, the northeastern USA suffered weather so cold that it was called "the year without a summer".

Fossilized Baryonyx

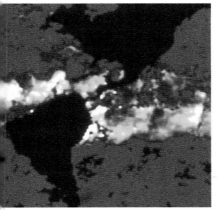

SPREADING CLOUDS
Once dust from volcanic eruptions gets into the stratosphere, high-level winds can quickly blow it far from its source. The dust from the 1982 eruption of El Chichón, Mexico, spread right around the world in just three weeks. This satellite picture shows that after Mount Pinatubo, in the Philippines, erupted on 15 June 1991, it took just 40 days for dust clouds to form around the globe.

VOLCANIC ODDITIES

VOLCANIC ACTIVITY often has spectacular results. The combination of immense heat, molten rock, sulphurous fumes, and mineral-rich water can produce a whole range of amazing landscapes, from pillars of salt to fire fountains.

Ancient plug of volcanic rock

Fountains of fiery magma

FIRE FOUNTAINS
The island of Réunion, in the Indian Ocean, is one of the largest volcanoes in the world. Its frequent eruptions of runny magma tend to be gentle, but the vents occasionally spout glowing fountains of red-hot lava into the air.

LE PUY, FRANCE
The church of Le Puy in France is perched on top of a precipitous rock 76 m (60 ft) high. This rock is the hardened inside of a volcanic vent from about two million years ago. The softer ash from the volcano around it has long since been worn away by the weather.

SMOKING VALLEY
In 1912, Mount Katmai, Alaska, erupted, emitting huge quantities of hot ash. Four years later, steam still billowed from cracks in the valley floor, so the area was named the Valley of Ten Thousand Smokes.

Ash 50 m (160 ft) deep fills the Valley of Ten Thousand Smokes

Water saturated with salts from volcanic rocks

Giant salt pillars grow up as water evaporates

KARUM SALT PILLARS

Among the strangest of all volcanic features are the Karum salt pillars in Ethiopia. These are made from salt washed out of volcanic rocks and into the shallow Assale Lake. The water evaporates in the hot sunshine, leaving the lake amazingly salty – so salty that the surface crystallizes, and pillars of salt can grow 3 m (10 ft) overnight.

Cement-like blocks formed from volcanic gases bubbling up through the ash

LANDSCAPE FACTS

• The Great Geyser in Iceland has to be stimulated into action with soap powder!

• Enormous colonies of clams, or "Clam Acres" feed on black smokers under the Pacific.

URGÜP CONES, TURKEY

Volcanic ash from an eruption is usually blown or washed gradually away, but occasionally it is cemented into weird shapes. At Urgüp, in central Turkey, ash was blown up into smokers, or tall chimneys, by gas fumes bubbling up from within the ash. These gradually hardened into outlandish pillars which were later dug out to make houses.

VOLCANOES IN SPACE

VOLCANOES HAVE PLAYED a major part in shaping the surfaces of all the rocky planets and moons in our solar system. The Earth's moon, for example, is covered with giant "seas", known as Maria. These are believed to be basaltic lava flows on a scale that dwarfs anything found on Earth.

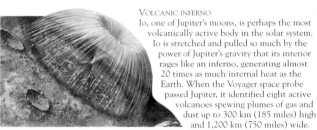

VOLCANIC INFERNO

Io, one of Jupiter's moons, is perhaps the most volcanically active body in the solar system. Io is stretched and pulled so much by the power of Jupiter's gravity that its interior rages like an inferno, generating almost 20 times as much internal heat as the Earth. When the Voyager space probe passed Jupiter, it identified eight active volcanoes spewing plumes of gas and dust up to 300 km (185 miles) high and 1,200 km (750 miles) wide.

OLYMPUS MONS

Mars' Olympus Mons is the biggest volcano in the solar system, at 25 km (15 miles) high and 600 km (375 miles) across. It is probably a hot-spot volcano, but as Mars has no moving plates, the hot spot continues to pump magma up in the same place, building up the volcano.

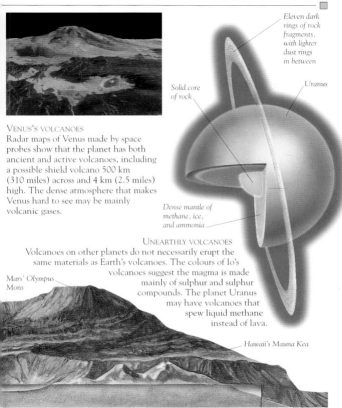

Eleven dark rings of rock fragments, with lighter dust rings in between

Uranus

Solid core of rock

Dense mantle of methane, ice, and ammonia

VENUS'S VOLCANOES

Radar maps of Venus made by space probes show that the planet has both ancient and active volcanoes, including a possible shield volcano 500 km (310 miles) across and 4 km (2.5 miles) high. The dense atmosphere that makes Venus hard to see may be mainly volcanic gases.

UNEARTHLY VOLCANOES

Volcanoes on other planets do not necessarily erupt the same materials as Earth's volcanoes. The colours of Io's volcanoes suggest the magma is made mainly of sulphur and sulphur compounds. The planet Uranus may have volcanoes that spew liquid methane instead of lava.

Mars' Olympus Mons

Hawaii's Mauna Kea

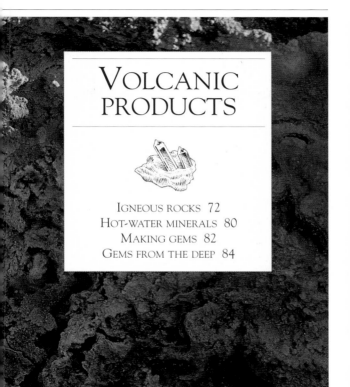

VOLCANIC PRODUCTS

IGNEOUS ROCKS

MOST OF THE EARTH'S crust is made up of igneous rocks, which are formed volcanically as molten magma solidifies. The other two main types of rock are sedimentary and metamorphic. All three types are linked by a continuous recycling of material called the rock cycle.

IGNEOUS ROCKS
Magma starts to cool as soon as it leaves the mantle, and crystals appear within the melt. The more it cools, the more crystals appear until eventually it turns into hard, crystalline, igneous rock.

METAMORPHIC ROCKS
Metamorphic rock is rock that has been transformed into a new state after being crushed by the forces that move tectonic plates, or seared by the intense heat of magma. This is immensely tough, and made of very fine crystals.

ROCK FACTS

• An old mountain range is made of roughly equal parts of all three rock types.

• A young mountain range is mostly igneous or metamorphic rock.

• Sedimentary rock often forms the bulk of coastal rocks.

SEDIMENTARY ROCKS
As thin layers of debris settle on the sea bed, they become compacted and cemented over millions of years into sedimentary rocks. Some, such as limestone, are made from plant or animal remains, or from chemicals settling out of water. Most are "clastic" – made from bits of rock worn away by the weather.

THE ROCK CYCLE

Lava and ash shoot high into the air

Clouds of dust and ash thrown into the atmosphere

Ash and fragments of rock fall in layers

Igneous rock weathers and erodes

Red hot magma rises to the Earth's surface and erupts in a volcano as lava

Igneous rock formed as lava cools

Sedimentary and metamorphic rock erodes

Layers compress into rock

Magma cools and hardens underground into plutonic igneous rock

Rock type altered by intense heat and pressure

Sedimentary rock

Melted rock forms magma

Metamorphic rock

Once hot enough, rock melts into magma

Igneous rock

Extrusive igneous rocks

Some igneous rock is called volcanic rock because it forms from lava spewed out by a volcano. It is also called extrusive igneous rock – in contrast to intrusive igneous rock, which forms when magma solidifies underground. Not all volcanic rock forms from lava; tuff is made from volcanic ash, and pumice is hardened lava froth. As the red-hot magma cools, crystals form in the rock.

HOW CRYSTALS FORM IN RHYOLITE

New lava flow

Lava too hot for crystals to form

1 Molten lava may initially be too hot for crystals to form, and runs like fluid over the landscape until the lava supply runs out, or until it begins to cool and slow down.

Surface of lava cools first

Feldspar crystals form first

2 As the lava flow slows, the surface layers begin to cool down. Small crystals of minerals with high melting points, such as feldspar, begin to grow inside the melt.

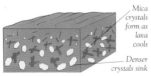

Mica crystals form as lava cools

Denser crystals sink

3 Deeper in the mix, where it takes longer to cool, feldspar crystals grow much bigger. As the lava cools, minerals such as mica crystallize into a different shape.

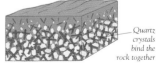

Quartz crystals bind the rock together

4 Eventually, as the lava cools still further, quartz begins to crystallize, but not in clusters like mica and feldspar. Instead, it fills in the gaps, binding the rock together.

Lava which cooled and cracked 60 million years ago

IGNEOUS ROCK FACTS
- 80 per cent of all volcanic rocks are basalt, and most are fine grained.
- Sticky dacite magmas (65 per cent silica) tend to form lava domes, like Mount St. Helens.

BASALT COLUMNS
The hexagonal columns of Fingal's Cave in Scotland are formed by "flood basalts", which can spill from fissures in the crust to form plateaus hundreds of metres deep.

Typical pinkish colour

Lighter colour than basalt

RHYOLITE
Pinkish rhyolite forms from the thick and sticky, highly acid, silica-rich (73 per cent) magma found in subduction zones. It piles up thickly around the vent after an explosive eruption.

ANDESITE
Similar in mineral content to basalt, but slightly richer in silica (55 per cent), andesite can form from block lava flows, similar to Hawaiian aa (see p. 42), but thicker and more slow-moving.

BASALT
Runny magmas with low silica (50 per cent) cool into dark-coloured basalt rock. The thin layers of such magmas, found along mid-ocean ridges, cool quickly, forming rock with fine crystals.

Intrusive igneous rocks

Rocks made from magma that hardens before it reaches the surface are called intrusive igneous rocks. Hypabyssal intrusions, such as dikes and sills, are small and form close to the surface, so they cool quite quickly to form medium-grained rocks. Plutonic intrusions such as batholiths are much larger, cooling slowly deep underground to form rocks with big, coarse crystal grains.

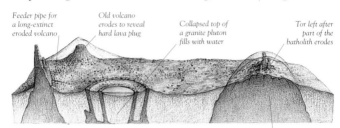

Feeder pipe for a long-extinct eroded volcano

Old volcano erodes to reveal hard lava plug

Collapsed top of a granite pluton fills with water

Tor left after part of the batholith erodes

IGNEOUS OUTCROPS
Granite forms entirely underground, yet is frequently seen on the surface because it is a tough rock that takes a long time to erode. Granite outcrops are often exposed when softer rock around them is eroded by weather and running water.

Part of a huge, dome-shaped batholith, or mass of lava, that has cooled beneath ground

	ACID ⟶				⟶ BASIC
VOLCANIC (FINE-GRAINED)	Rhyolite	Dacite	Trachyte	Andesite	Basalt
HYPABYSSAL (MEDIUM-GRAINED)	Quartz				Dolerite
PLUTONIC (COARSE-GRAINED)	Granite		Syenite	Diorite	Gabbro

CRYSTAL SIZE IN ROCK
The quicker lava cools, the finer grained the resulting rock is. Intrusive igneous rocks are almost always coarser than those that cool on the surface. Plutonic rock is the coarsest of all.

GRANITE
The commonest plutonic rock, granite is found in big domes where tectonic plates crunch together to form mountains. This light-coloured rock forms from acidic, thick, silica-rich rhyolitic magma.

DIORITE
The coarse-grained, plutonic equivalent of andesite is diorite. It is formed when contact with other rocks adds impurities to the granitic magma, often in minor intrusions, such as dikes.

GABBRO
Gabbro is the most common plutonic rock after granite. It is the coarse-grained, underground equivalent of basaltic rock, and forms in igneous intrusions called lopoliths.

Finer grains of older lava

Coarser grains of newer granite

XENOLITHS
When magma solidifies to make new igneous rock, it often traps fragments of old "foreign" rock called xenoliths. These may be partly changed, or metamorphosed, by heat and pressure.

FACTBOX
• The grains in hypabyssal rocks measure 1–5 mm (0.2–0.4 in).

• The grains in plutonic rocks measure 5 mm (0.4 in) or more.

Metamorphic rocks

The immense heat and pressure created by earthquakes and volcanic activity can dramatically change rock shapes. Baked by magma or squeezed by tectonic activity, this transformation to metamorphic rock can take place on a local or regional scale.

MARBLE DAVID
Marble, a beautiful rock, is a form of metamorphosed limestone. The most famous type, Carrara marble, is found in Italy, where Michelangelo (1475–1564) used it to sculpt his statue of David.

CONTACT METAMORPHISM
When rocks are altered by direct contact with hot magma – such as an igneous intrusion – the change is known as contact metamorphism.

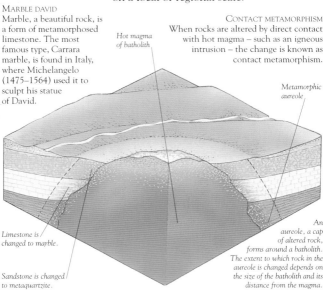

Hot magma of batholith

Metamorphic aureole

Limestone is changed to marble.

Sandstone is changed to metaquartzite.

An aureole, a cap of altered rock, forms around a batholith. The extent to which rock in the aureole is changed depends on the size of the batholith and its distance from the magma.

High-grade metamorphism: gneiss   Medium-grade metamorphism: schist

Low-grade metamorphism: slate

REGIONAL METAMORPHISM

Rocks can be altered as they are crushed and baked under mountain ranges thrown up by colliding tectonic plates. Intense pressure can give rocks a "foliated", or layered texture, and crystals reform in a banded pattern known as schistosity. Rocks at the heart of the activity undergo high-grade metamorphism – the most intense folding. Those further away experience low-grade change.

> ### METAMORPHIC FACTS
> • Quartz and kaolinite meld into pyrophyllite above 300°C (572°F).
> • Over 400°C (752°F) pyrophillite turns to andalusite or kyanite.

SLATE

Slate is a dark, grey, flaky rock, formed by low-grade regional metamorphism from mudstone and shale. Extensive pressure changes clay and quartz minerals into smooth, flat layers.

SCHIST

When medium-grade regional metamorphism affects shale and mudstone, foliated metamorphic rock forms. The minerals recrystallize into chlorite, biotite mica, and garnet.

GNEISS

When mudstone, slate, or schists are subject to high-grade regional metamorphism, a mottled rock called gneiss forms. Within this rock, bands of dark new minerals alternate with lighter bands of quartz and feldspar.

MARBLE

Generally made by contact or regional metamorphism of limestone, marble can also be made from other rocks. Heat and pressure change the calcite in the limestone into sugary marble.

HOT-WATER MINERALS

CHEMICAL-RICH water circulates underground in hydrothermal systems. Washed through cracks to cooler places, chemicals such as sulphur and copper solidify over thousands of years to form valuable mineral deposits.

SULPHUROUS FUMES
One of the most common substances in hot volcanic liquids and fumes is sulphur. Steam bubbling through a fumarole has the unmistakable bad-egg smell of hydrogen sulphide. Spiky sulphur crystals form at the mouth of the vent.

A gas mask protects against sulphur dioxide fumes

ACID ATTACK
Liquids and gases pouring from volcanoes are rich in chemicals because the heat vapourizes or dissolves many substances. Gas masks are needed where there are acidic gases such as sulphur dioxide. Some crater lakes, like Kawah Idjen in Java, (right) are full of acid.

SULPHUR FACTS
• Sulphur is added
to rubber to make it
tougher – a process
called vulcanization.
• Sulphur and other
gases are still belching
from Kawah Idjen,
40 years after its last
eruption.

MINERALS FROM THE DEEP
Black smokers gave the first clue to the riches of
hydrothermal deposits, covering the sea bed either
side of mid-ocean ridges with valuable compounds of
sulphur, including the ores of copper, zinc, and iron.

*Sulphur crystals range
from transparent to
translucent*

SULPHUR
CRYSTALS
As volcanic vapours
cool, the sulphur they
hold slowly precipitates to
form crystals. Under the right
conditions, large yellow crystals grow,
like those mined for centuries in Sicily.

MAKING GEMS

CRYSTALS FORM as hot magma cools. Minerals with the highest melting points crystallize first, changing the melt's chemical mix. As the last of the melt crystallizes, rocks called pegmatites form, which may contain rare gems.

Amethyst crystal

Iron gives the amethyst its purple colour

AMETHYST
Quartz is a common constituent of igneous rocks, but in pegmatites, it often forms gems such as rose quartz, citrine quartz, and, less commonly, purple amethyst.

Pegmatite – rock formed from the last of the melt

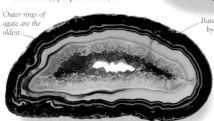

Outer rings of agate are the oldest

Bands coloured by oxides and hydroxides of iron

AGATE BUBBLE
Some of the best crystals are formed in bubbles in the magma called geodes. Hot water, enriched by minerals from the magma, trickles through the rock to fill the geodes. As they crystallize they form gems, such as agate.

CRYSTAL FACTS

• A spodumene crystal 15 m (50 ft) long was found in the Black hills of South Dakota.

• A beryl crystal 10 m (33 ft) long turned up in the Bumpus Quarry near Bethel, Maine.

MASSIVE QUARTZ

Iron oxides produce orange colour

TIGER'S EYE
Massive quartz is composed of tiny grains or fibres. Sometimes, flecks of new minerals may replace the original minerals within the crystals. In stripy tiger's eye, tiny quartz crystals replace asbestos fibres.

Colour effect called chatoyancy

POLISHED TIGER'S EYE

The brighter the green, the more precious the stone

CHRYSOPRASE
When quartz cools slowly in a cavity, it can form solid masses of the fine-grained gem chalcedony; the most valuable form is bright green chrysoprase.

Interlocking quartz crystals are arranged in a random mass

JASPER
Another form of chalcedony is jasper, which often forms in bubbles in cool lavas. Traces of iron oxide turn it red, and actinolite or chlorite turn it green.

Traces of iron oxide produce warm shades of red and orange

GEMS FROM THE DEEP

MANY VALUABLE GEMS form from
magma by crystallization. These
gems, such as ruby, sapphire, spinel,
olivine, pyrope garnet, and zircon
have high melting points and simple
chemical compositions. Diamond,
made of pure carbon, is the
simplest and toughest of all.

ECLOGITE
As the basalt of a
subducted ocean crust is
pushed into the Earth's
interior, heat and
pressure transforms it into
the rock eclogite. The
carbon that makes
diamond probably came
from sediments dragged
down along with the
ocean crust.

Diamond

DIAMOND
Diamond is the
hardest naturally
occuring mineral.
Diamonds are found in
veins of the rare igneous rocks
kimberlite and lamproite. Measurements show
that they are often more than three billion years older
than the kimberlites which bring them to the surface.

EMERALD
The finest emeralds, a form of beryl, come from the Muzo
and Chivor mines in Colombia. They are formed from
mineral-rich brine trapped in cavities in limestone,
distorted by the movement of tectonic plates.

SAPPHIRE

Sapphire is one of many hard gems that crystallize at high temperatures deep in the Earth's interior. Sapphire is the blue gem form of the mineral corundum, tinted by iron and titanium. The deep cornflower blue sapphires from Kashmir are the most valued.

RUBY

Another form of corundum, rubies sometimes form deep in the Earth from magma. However, the most famous rubies – the fabulous gems from the Mogok area of Myanmar – were made when minerals containing aluminium recrystallized under extreme heat and pressure.

BERYL

Traces of manganese turn beryl pink (morganite) and red; iron turns it blue (aquamarine) and yellow (heliodore); and chromium or vanadium turns it green (emerald). Beryl usually crystallizes in granitic pegmatites, but may also form when rocks are metamorphosed.

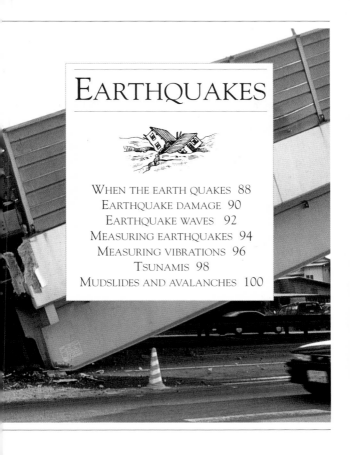

EARTHQUAKES

WHEN THE EARTH QUAKES

EVERY DAY SOME PART of the world is shaken by an earthquake. Some are barely strong enough to rock a cradle, while others are so violent they can destroy cities. Most occur in earthquake zones, which coincide with the cracks between tectonic plates, and are triggered by the immense forces generated as plates grind together.

HOW AN EARTHQUAKE IS GENERATED
When one plate drags past another, the rock bends and stretches either side of the crack and eventually snaps. This rupture sends shock waves, known as seismic waves, through the ground at 20 times the speed of sound, so there is little warning of the impending quake. These waves radiate from the hypocentre, gradually diminishing in intensity.

EARTHQUAKE FACTS
• The major San Andreas fault lies along 965 km (600 miles) of California's coast.
• The 1906 Los Angeles earthquake killed 3,000 people and left a further 250,000 homeless.

The epicentre is the point on the surface where waves are strongest, directly above the hypocentre

The hypocentre, or focus, is the centre of the earthquake below ground

SHOCK SEQUENCE
In most quakes, a few minor tremors
(foreshocks) are followed by an
intense burst, then a second series
of minor tremors (aftershocks)
over the next hour or so. The
main shock may last just a
few minutes, but a violent
quake is enough to bring
down tall buildings.

BIG THUMPER
By tracing earthquake
vibrations, seismologists
learn about the rocks
underground. A
vibroseis truck
thumps the ground,
creating artificial
shock waves.
Seismographs
then pick up
a wave
pattern that
reveals rock
structures.

*Isoseismic lines show
where the quake's
intensity is equal*

*Other fault lines along
which earthquakes could
potentially occur*

EARTHQUAKE DAMAGE

MANY OF THE WORLD'S major cities, including
Los Angeles, Mexico, and Tokyo, are located in
major earthquake zones. The people that live
in these places learn to cope with minor tremors.
But sooner or later, a major city may be
hit by a large earthquake,
causing widespread
destruction and death.

*In 1906, a major quake struck San Francisco,
shaking the city for 3 minutes. In a short time,
many fires had started, fuelled by gas leaks.*

*Buildings
collapse as
the ground
shakes*

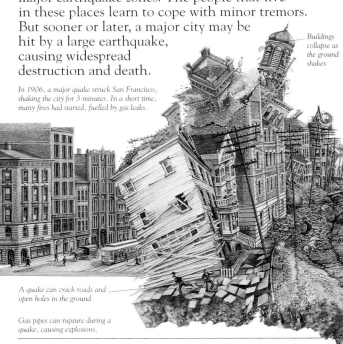

*A quake can crack roads and
open holes in the ground*

*Gas pipes can rupture during a
quake, causing explosions.*

SHAKY GROUND

The extent of damage an earthquake causes depends on the distance of a city from the epicentre of the quake, and on the type of ground it is built on. Loose sediments can magnify a strong quake; in the 1995 earthquake in Kobe, Japan, buildings built on landfill sustained the worst damage.

Fires that are caused by the quake are kept burning, fanned by the wind

In the San Francisco quake of 1906 streetcars ground to a halt as rails buckled. Over 400 km (250 miles) of railway track was destroyed in and around the city.

EARTHQUAKE WAVES

TWO MAIN KINDS of shock wave are generated by an earthquake. Body waves travel underground at great speeds, and often pass right around the world. Much slower surface waves move out along the ground from the epicentre, but can cause far more damage.

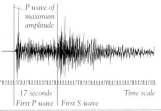

P wave of maximum amplitude

17 seconds | Time scale
First P wave | First S wave

TIME LAG
Seismograph readings show the arrival pattern of different body waves in a quake. P waves arrive first, S waves are slower. The time lag between the two, in this case 17 seconds, indicates how far away the focus is. The measurement on the Richter scale (see pp. 94–95) is the P wave with the maximum amplitude.

BODY WAVES

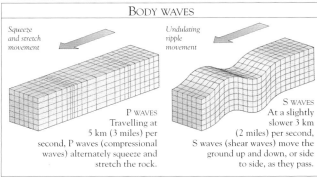

Squeeze and stretch movement

Undulating ripple movement

P WAVES
Travelling at 5 km (3 miles) per second, P waves (compressional waves) alternately squeeze and stretch the rock.

S WAVES
At a slightly slower 3 km (2 miles) per second, S waves (shear waves) move the ground up and down, or side to side, as they pass.

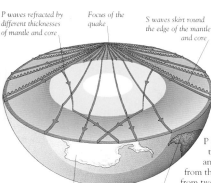

P waves refracted by different thicknesses of mantle and core

Focus of the quake

S waves skirt round the edge of the mantle and core

S waves are repelled by liquid core but P waves pass straight through

Shadow zone, where it is impossible to detect earthquake waves

ALL AROUND THE WORLD
P waves can travel right around the world in just over an hour, and register on seismographs far from the quake. Comparing readouts from two or three stations pinpoints a quake's location. The way the different waves are refracted, or bent, through the Earth reveals much about its interior.

SURFACE WAVES

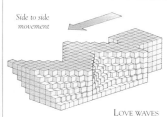

Side to side movement

Up and down wave-like movement

LOVE WAVES
Love, or Q waves shake the ground from side to side in a jerky movement that is devastating to tall buildings.

RAYLEIGH WAVES
Rayleigh, or R waves shake the ground up and down, often creating a visible rolling and billowing of the ground.

EARTHQUAKE MEASUREMENT

THE RICHTER SCALE uses seismograph readings to assess how bad a quake is, while the Modified Mercalli scale records the quake's destructive effects. Both these scales are being superceded by Moment-magnitude, which combines Richter readings with observations of rock movements.

MERCALLI SCALE

On a scale of I to XII, the Mercalli scale, devised by Giuseppe Mercalli (1850–1914), indicates a quake's intensity in a fixed place by observing its effects. A quake weakens away from its epicentre, so the Mercalli rating varies according to where it is assessed.

I Movement detected by instruments
II Felt by people resting
III Hanging lights sway
IV Plates and windows rattle, parked cars rock

V Buildings tremble, liquids spill; vibrations felt by most people
VI Movement felt by all, pictures fall off walls, window glass shatters

VII Bricks and tiles fall, chimneys crack, difficult to stand
VIII Hard to steer a car, tree branches snap, chimneys fall

IX General panic, ground cracks, mud oozes from ground
X Pipes burst, rivers flood, most buildings collapse

XI Bridges collapse, railways lines buckle, landslides occur
XII Near total destruction, rivers change course, waves ripple ground

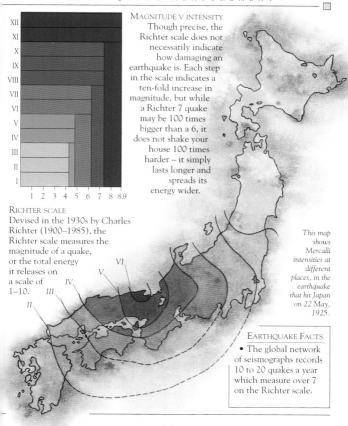

MAGNITUDE V INTENSITY

Though precise, the Richter scale does not necessarily indicate how damaging an earthquake is. Each step in the scale indicates a ten-fold increase in magnitude, but while a Richter 7 quake may be 100 times bigger than a 6, it does not shake your house 100 times harder – it simply lasts longer and spreads its energy wider.

RICHTER SCALE

Devised in the 1930s by Charles Richter (1900–1985), the Richter scale measures the magnitude of a quake, or the total energy it releases on a scale of 1–10.

This map shows Mercalli intensities at different places, in the earthquake that hit Japan on 22 May, 1925.

EARTHQUAKE FACTS

• The global network of seismographs records 10 to 20 quakes a year which measure over 7 on the Richter scale.

MEASURING VIBRATIONS

THE SIZE of an earthquake can be measured by an instrument called a seismometer. The part of a seismometer that records earthquake vibrations is the seismograph, and the written trace of the vibrations is the seismogram. This device is derived from the seismoscope, invented 1,700 years earlier by Chinese scholar Zhang Heng.

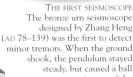

THE FIRST SEISMOSCOPE
The bronze urn seismoscope designed by Zhang Heng (AD 78–139) was the first to detect minor tremors. When the ground shook, the pendulum stayed steady, but caused a ball in one of the dragons' mouths around the top of the urn to fall.

The direction of the earthquake is indicated by which ball drops into the mouth of which frog below.

Pendulum

Clock stops when shaking starts

Clock records frequency of vibrations

Recorder connected electrically to a separate seismometer

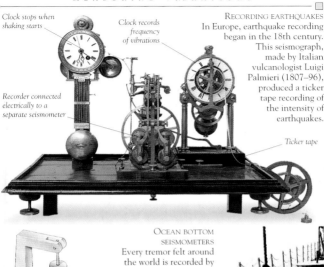

RECORDING EARTHQUAKES

In Europe, earthquake recording began in the 18th century. This seismograph, made by Italian vulcanologist Luigi Palmieri (1807–96), produced a ticker tape recording of the intensity of earthquakes.

Ticker tape

SEISMOGRAPH

In a basic seismograph, the hanging weight stays still as the rest of the device shakes. A pen attached to the weight traces the shakes on paper. Today, the shakes are recorded electronically.

OCEAN BOTTOM SEISMOMETERS

Every tremor felt around the world is recorded by a linked network of synchronized seismometers. The waves from any quake can be traced around the globe and the focus pinpointed, so that the earthquake can be rated on the Richter scale. Now waterproof Ocean Bottom Seismometers are able to record vibrations on the ocean floor.

TSUNAMIS

WHEN THE sea bed is shaken by an earthquake or volcano, the vibrations set off waves that roll along as fast as a jet plane – 700 km/h (435 mph). In deep water, tsunamis are hard to detect, but in shallow coastal waters, they rear up into giant, destructive waves.

Tsunami reaches Japan in 24 hours

WAVE RISK
Tsunamis can travel over wide expanses of ocean. In 1960, an earthquake in Chile caused a tsunami that devastated the Japanese coast 24 hours later.

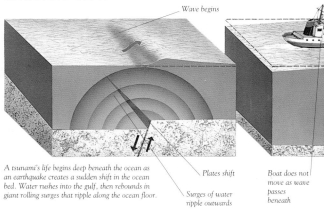

Wave begins

A tsunami's life begins deep beneath the ocean as an earthquake creates a sudden shift in the ocean bed. Water rushes into the gulf, then rebounds in giant rolling surges that ripple along the ocean floor.

Plates shift

Surges of water ripple outwards

Boat does not move as wave passes beneath

Just before a tsunami, sea level falls

Tsunami engulfs land for up to five minutes

Tsunamis can change the shape of the coastline

TSUNAMI TRAIN

Tsunamis generally occur in trains of 12 or more, from five minutes to an hour apart. They can engulf lowland coasts for up to five minutes.

Swift and devastating, tsunamis can sweep away entire villages before sucking debris, and even the land itself, back out to sea.

Wave rears up

TSUNAMI FACTS

• The highest recorded tsunami, 84 m (278 ft), hit Japan in 1971.

• In 1883, a tsunami set off by Krakatoa swept a ship 2.6 km (1.5 miles) inland.

In deep water, these fast-moving rolls are almost invisible on the surface, barely rocking a boat as they pass underneath it.

In shallower water, huge waves 30 m (98 ft) high appear. As the first arrives, the beach water is sucked away before the wave hits.

MUDSLIDES AND AVALANCHES

BOTH EARTHQUAKES and volcanoes can trigger off mudslides and avalanches. Often these are minor, but sometimes they send tons of rock, mud, or snow onto villages and towns, a peril even more deadly than the original eruption or quake itself.

KILLER MUD
Volcanoes create mudflows called "lahars" when fragments of rock and ash mix with water, resulting in a slurry that can surge down steep valleys at speeds of 30–40 km/h (19–25 mph).

WATER UNLEASHED
Shock waves during a quake may cause high dams to crack and burst and rivers to change course. The ensuing floods cause damage and death.

People escape in boats

Victims climb on roofs

DISASTER FACTS
• On Mount Usu, Japan, mudflows are redirected by check dams and conduits.

• A quake in 1970 in the Andes set off a rock and ice avalanche, killing 18,000 people.

TYPES OF SNOW AVALANCHE

SLAB AVALANCHE

Earthquakes in snowy mountain regions often set off slab avalanches. A slab of unstable layers of ice and snow that have built up during alternate freezes and thaws crashes down, breaking up as it falls.

LOOSE SNOW

Dry, loose snow often occurs after a heavy fall. It slides along the ground and usually comes to rest quickly. It can turn into an airborne powder avalanche if disturbed by the vibrations of an earthquake.

WET SNOW

In spring, wet snow avalanches are a hazard. Snow becomes saturated with water and moves slowly downhill. Even a minor eruption of a snow-capped volcano may set off this kind of snowslide.

POWDER SNOW

When fresh snow falls, it may slide downhill as it builds up. But an earthquake can trigger a powder avalanche, which bowls down the slope compressing air in front of it and creating a destructive shock wave.

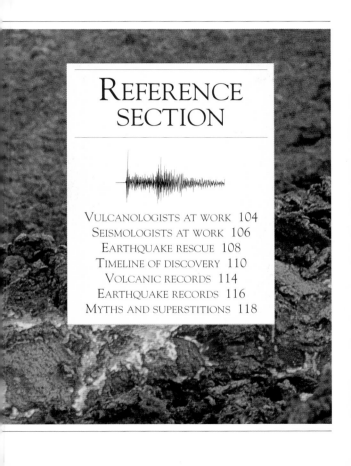

REFERENCE SECTION

VULCANOLOGISTS AT WORK

VULCANOLOGISTS STUDY volcanoes to find out when they will erupt. With volcanoes that show persistent eruption patterns, the best way to forecast eruptions is to study past behaviour. But the most dangerous explosive volcanoes are also the most erratic, and need constant monitoring.

Metal-coated protective suit reflects heat but inhibits movement

HAT AND GLOVE
When scientists need to examine a volcano at close range, a hard hat, asbestos gloves, and a heatproof suit are essential.

Hard hat

Heat-resistant asbestos gloves

LOOKING FOR CLUES
A crucial sign of an imminent eruption seems to be a build-up of magma beneath the volcano. Tell-tale signs of this include increases in ground temperature, rising levels of carbon dioxide in bore-holes, and changes in gravity or variations in magnetic or electrical fields.

HOT ROD

Occasionally, vulcanologists need to take
samples of red-hot lava directly from the
lava stream. This is a dangerous task, but
a metal rod helps. From as safe a place
as possible, the vulcanologist dips the
pronged end of the rod into the lava flow
and twists it. The prongs hook a blob of
lava out of the stream.

Light, portable tiltmeter

Spirit level

WATCHING FOR SWELLING

Vulcanologists use hand surveying tools
like mining transit tools to make rapid
maps and watch for any changes in the
volcano's slope, such as swelling caused
by the build-up of magma. These may
not always be accurate enough.

Rotating stage

MINING TRANSIT TOOL

Folding portable tripod

Twisted prongs trap lava

THE QUEST FOR ACCURACY

Tiltmeters use lasers to
show variations in the
fluid level that may
reveal slight changes in
the volcanic slope. Space
satellites make the task
safer and more acccurate.
Stations near many
volcanoes use the Global
Positioning System (GPS)
to detect slight lateral
movements. Other
satellites use "radar
interferometry" to make
accurate maps of
dangerous volcanoes.

SEISMOLOGISTS AT WORK

MOST SEISMOLOGISTS BELIEVE that the key to predicting earthquakes is to look for strain building in rocks. Precision surveys search for signs of rocks changing shape, using tiltmeters on the ground and satellites in space by rangefinding with laser beams. The more detectable the movement, the less likely it is to lead to a big quake.

THE EARTHQUAKE RECORD
Studying past quakes may help scientists to predict the next big tremor. If there has not been a quake for some time, strain will have built up. Big quakes are likely to occur at 'seismic' gaps, where not even minor tremors have occured.

Where quakes are common, children are trained to shelter under a bed or heavy table until tremors pass

EARTHQUAKE DRILL
In areas prone to quakes, earthquake drills are a part of life. People are well prepared, so that they can get to safety even if a quake strikes at night.

SHAKE TESTING
In 1923, Tokyo, Japan, was destroyed by a quake. When the city was rebuilt that year, the Japanese invented this shaking table to test models of new buildings for stability. Today, shake tables are computer-operated.

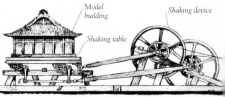

Model building

Shaking device

Shaking table

EARTHQUAKE-PROOFING

Most deaths in earthquakes are caused by collapsing buildings and roadways. So in earthquake-prone cities such as San Francisco and Tokyo, all new building follows safety guidelines. Regulations insist on deep, firm foundations of steel and concrete.

STILL STANDING
Earthquake proofing is not a new idea – the Japanese have practised it for years. This ancient wooden Buddhist pagoda is still standing because its central column was built to absorb tremors.

TRANSAMERICA PYRAMID
Tall buildings are not suitable for earthquake zones, but San Fransisco's distinctive Transamerica Pyramid incorporates many earthquake safety design features. It was built to be twice as strong as regulations require, with a wide, pyramid base designed to reduce potential swaying by up to a third.

LATEST DESIGNS
The Japanese are trying to redesign elevated roadways, which can collapse in a quake. Engineers in Tokyo are experimenting with rubber cushions to place under the pillars of the Kajima Construction, to dampen the vibrations.

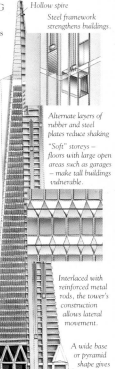

Hollow spire

Steel framework strengthens buildings.

Alternate layers of rubber and steel plates reduce shaking

"Soft" storeys – floors with large open areas such as garages – make tall buildings vulnerable.

Interlaced with reinforced metal rods, the tower's construction allows lateral movement.

A wide base or pyramid shape gives extra stability.

EARTHQUAKE RESCUE

IN THE AFTERMATH of a big earthquake or volcanic
eruption, it is vital to rescue victims quickly. Some
may be killed during the event itself, while others
die later from injuries caused by the disaster. Many
victims need to be pulled out from beneath the debris,
so the rescuer's task can be difficult and dangerous.

HEAT-SEEKING
Locating wounded or unconscious
victims under mountains of
rubble is made easier with
thermal imaging cameras.
These cameras are sensitive
to infrared radiation – the
radiation of heat. They pick
up the heat of living bodies,
even in pitch darkness. The
problem is distinguishing
bodies from other heat
sources. The best time to
look is early in the morning
when background heat is lowest.

UNSTABLE SHELTER
When a quake strikes, tall, unstable
buildings can crash to the ground in
minutes, burying their inhabitants in
collapsed masonry. In this quake on the
Peloponnese in Greece, many
buildings were reduced to rubble.

RESCUE FROM ABOVE
Earthquakes disrupt communications and can make it difficult for rescue services to get close enough to help. The helicopter is invaluable in these situations, and is used to pluck survivors from dangerous situations and to drop vital supplies and medical equipment.

TRAPPED PERSON DETECTOR
Although thermal imaging cameras spot bodies in darkness, they cannot "see" through solid material. This sensitive equipment works by detecting slight vibrations and sounds. It was first used to locate survivors after the Armenian quake of 1988.

Rescuer uses headphones to pick up human sounds

Microphone so rescuer can talk to survivor

Yellow one-way electrode picks up vibrations

Red two-way electrode lets rescuer hear survivor

TIMELINE OF DISCOVERY

THE THREAT OF VOLCANIC ACTIVITY to cities around the world has encouraged individuals to observe volcanoes and earthquakes from the earliest times. Their discoveries are the base of our knowledge today.

ARISTOTLE 384–322BC
The Greek philosopher and naturalist Aristotle, whose ideas dominated European thought for 2,000 years, was one of the first to study earthquakes scientifically. He believed that they were caused when air trapped in deep underground pockets escaped to the surface.

ZHANG HENG 78–139BC
A Chinese imperial historian and astronomer born in Nanyang, Zhang Heng made the first seismoscope to record earthquakes. He also realized that moonlight comes from the Sun, long before his Western counterparts, and that lunar eclipses occurred when the Earth's shadow fell on the moon.

AVICENNA 980–1037
Born near Bokhara, Turkey, Avicenna was a renowned physician to numerous Persian sultans and known for his prodigious learning. Among his 200 or so books on scientific topics was *Liber de Mineralibus*, his ideas on earthquakes and geology which dominated thinking for 500 years.

ATHENASIUS KIRCHER 1602–1680
The German Jesuit thinker, Kircher, was a great 17th-century science writer, also famous throughout Europe for his translations of Egyptian hieroglyphs. His book *Mundus Subterraneus* (*The Subterranean World*) showed how Earth's fiery core feeds volcanoes and heated thermal springs.

BENOIT DE MAILLET 1656–1738
A French diplomat and traveller, de Maillet wrote a book about the Earth's history called *Telliamed* (his name spelled backwards). He was one of the first to realize that Earth is very old. Two hundred years before anyone else, he argued that it was more than two billion years old. But he also believed that volcanoes were pockets of oil and fats from animals and fishes that had become trapped in sedimentary rock and had caught fire.

JOHN-ETIENNE GUETTARD 1715–1766
A natural scientist, Guettard insisted on drawing his conclusions from direct observation only, and made numerous field trips to identify rocks. He made the first geological map of France and astounded French scientists by proving that there were once active volcanoes in the Massif Central, central France.

NICHOLAS DESMAREST 1725–1615
A quiet bureaucrat whose hobby was geology, Desmarest studied volcanic rocks in the French Auvergne. While Guettard and other geologists believed that basalts were sedimentary rock, Desmarest showed that they were lava flows which, once cooled, formed the region's amazing hexagonal columns.

JAMES HUTTON 1726–1797
Scottish geologist James Hutton is considered the founder of modern geology. In Hutton's day, most people believed the Earth was just a few thousand years old. But he showed that it was much, much older and that the landscape had been shaped gradually over millions of years. He was the first person to realize that intrusive igneous rocks such as granite were once molten rock that had emerged from deep inside the Earth.

ABRAHAM WERNER 1750–1817
German geologist Werner was one of the "superstars" of 18th-century geology and people would listen to his lectures spellbound. He believed volcanoes were underground veins of coal that had caught fire and burned their way to the surface, and were insignificant geographically . Students of his – Jean d'Aubuisson, Leopold von Buch, and Alexander von Humboldt – later came to realize that he was wrong.

JAMES HALL 1761–1832
Scotsman Hall, a friend of Hutton, studied the volcanoes of Italy. Many 18th-century geologists believed that the presence of crystals in igneous rocks proved that they had never been molten. Hall tested rocks in a hot iron foundry and showed that molten basalt forms crystals if cooled slowly.

ALEXANDER VON HUMBOLDT 1769–1859
One of the great scientific explorers of the 19th century, German Baron Humboldt went on epic expeditions to South America collecting data. He studied American volcanoes, and realized that they coincided with geological faults. He also realized that many rocks are igneous.

GEORGE SCROPE 1801–1875
An English gentleman and Member of Parliament, Scrope developed a passionate interest in volcanoes after visiting the Italian volcanoes Stromboli and Etna. In 1825, he published *Considerations on Volcanoes*, in which he put forward the idea that explosive eruptions were driven by the expansion of gases within magma. He later realized that the most important of these gases was water vapour.

LUIGI PALMIERI 1807–1896
Italian scientist Luigi Palmieri realized while observing the eruption of Italy's Mount Vesuvius in 1855 that an instrument that could detect very faint tremors in the ground might help predict both earthquakes and volcanic eruptions. To detect these tremors, he built the first true seismograph in 1855. He became a national hero when he stayed at his observatory throughout an eruption on Vesuvius in 1872.

ROBERT MALLET 1810–1881
An Irish civil engineer, Mallet became interested in earthquakes and volcanoes after studying an eruption of Vesuvius in 1857. He tried to work out how fast earthquake waves travel and made a map of earthquakes which showed, for the first time, that earthquakes occur in particular zones.

GIUSEPPE MERCALLI 1850–1914
An Italian professor of natural sciences, Mercalli was a pioneer in earthquake studies, observing in detail the progress of tremors in the major earthquake districts of Italy. He is best known for the scale of earthquake intensity, which he devised first in 1897 and modified several times.

JOHN MILNE 1850–1913
A British mining engineer and professor of Geology and Mining at Tokyo University, Milne was interested in seismographs, quakes, and earthquake-proofing of buildings. His own reliable and sensitive seismograph was the first to record very distant earthquakes.

FRANK ALVORD PERRET 1857–1940
American vulcanologist Perret was a pioneer of eruption prediction. Working on Vesuvius in 1906, he predicted an eruption based on a buzzing sound – the harmonic vibration of the magma mass. Using microphones to pick up vibrations he also studied Mount Pelée, Martinique.

THOMAS JAGGER JUNIOR 1871–1953
A firm believer in on-the-spot study of volcanoes,
American vulcanologist Jagger was the first to set up
a permanent volcano observation post, on the island
of Hawaii, in 1912. Since that time, the Hawaiian
Volcano Observatory has made Hawaii's Kilauea the
most thoroughly studied and understood volcano in
the world. It also pioneered the use of bombing in
order to divert lava flows.

ALFRED WEGENER 1880–1930
German meteorologist Wegener was
the first to seriously propose the idea
of continental drift, and that all the
continents had once been joined in
one "supercontinent" called Pangaea.
His ideas were ridiculed, despite
evidence such as matching rock strata
across widely separated continents.

ALFRED LACROIX (1863–1948)
Lacroix arrived in Martinique on June
23, 1902, straight after the eruption of
Mount Pelée, and published his report
on the volcano nine months later. It
became a vulcanology classic, clearly
describing the *nuée ardente*, or
glowing cloud, which was so deadly
for the citizens of St Pierre.

CHARLES RICHTER 1900–1985
In California in the 1930s, Richter, a
seismologist, found a way to compare
the size of local quakes. By measuring
the size of peaks for each earthquake
on a seismograph and the distance of
their focus, he devised the Richter
scale, a complete scale for quake
magnitude that is still standard today.

KIYOO WADATI 1902–1996
In 1927, Japanese seismologist Wadati
showed that many earthquakes start
in subduction zones deep in the
Earth's crust – at least 300 km (185
miles) down. When American Hugo
Benioff (1899–1968) noted that the
zones lie near ocean trenches, they
were named Benioff-Wadati zones.

HAROUN TAZIEFF 1914–1998
Tazieff, who was born in Poland and worked in
France, was a "superstar" of 20th-century
vulcanology. Having investigated many of the world's
major volcanoes, he was appointed the first French
Secretary of State for the Prevention of Natural and
Technological Disasters in 1984. His stance at that
time on evacuation in advance of potential eruptions
was considered controversial.

VOLCANIC RECORDS

SOME FEATURES of volcanic activity, such as cone-shaped peaks, crater lakes, and recent lava flows are unmistakable. Every inch of the Earth's surface has been affected by volcanic activity at some time, even if all signs of it have been eroded by the passage of billions of years.

• 130–80 million years ago, in the age of dinosaurs, huge flows of basalt lava – called flood basalts – oozed from the floors of the Pacific and Indian Oceans.

• 60–65 million years ago, basalt gushed onto the surface in an almost continuous flow to form India's Deccan plateau.

• 17 million years ago, huge molten basalt flows from a hot spot created the Columbia plateau in Oregon and Washington.

• 2 million years ago, one of the biggest eruptions ever took place in Yellowstone, Wyoming. Enough magma poured on to the surface to build half a dozen Mount Fujiyamas.

• 1645 BC Greek island of Thera erupted, burying the Minoan city of Akroteri, perhaps giving rise to the Atlantis myth.

• AD 79 Vesuvius erupted, burying the ancient Roman town of Pompeii.

• AD 186 Lake Taupo, New Zealand, was created in a vast eruption.

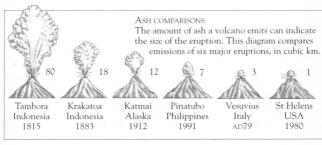

ASH COMPARISONS
The amount of ash a volcano emits can indicate the size of the eruption. This diagram compares emissions of six major eruptions, in cubic km.

80	18	12	7	3	1
Tambora Indonesia 1815	Krakatoa Indonesia 1883	Katmai Alaska 1912	Pinatubo Philippines 1991	Vesuvius Italy AD79	St Helens USA 1980

• AD 300 An eruption in El Salvador left a caldera – now Lake Ilopango. Survivors of the eruption may have founded the Mayan civilization.

• 1669 Mount Etna, Sicily, Europe's largest volcano, erupted, burying the town of Catania in lava.

• 1783 Laki mountain, in Iceland, poured out lava and gases. These gases killed crops, and a fifth of Iceland's people starved.

• 1815 Tambora erupted in Indonesia, sending dust clouds around the globe and dimming the sun.

• 1902 St Pierre, on Martinique, was destroyed by burning clouds of dust from Mount Pelée.

• 1963 The volcanic island of Surtsey appeared off the coast of Iceland.

• 1980 Mount St Helens, in Washington, USA, erupted, flattening forests.

• 1986 Gases from Lake Nyos, Cameroon, killed thousands but left houses and gardens undamaged.

• 1991 Eruption of Mount Pinatubo, the Philippines, the biggest this century.

• 1996 Grímsvötn, Iceland, erupted under the Vatnajökull glacier, melting huge quantities of ice.

• 1997 Much of the island of Montserrat was devastated by an eruption.

VOLCANIC PEAKS

Many high peaks are volcanic. There are more than ten volcanoes over 7,000 m (22,966 ft) high in the Andes. Below is a comparison of some volcanic peaks with Everest, the world's highest mountain.

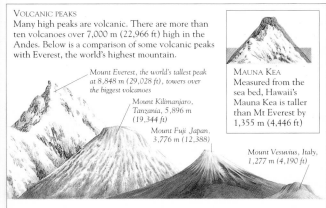

Mount Everest, the world's tallest peak at 8,848 m (29,028 ft), towers over the biggest volcanoes

Mount Kilimanjaro, Tanzania, 5,896 m (19,344 ft)

Mount Fuji, Japan, 3,776 m (12,388)

MAUNA KEA Measured from the sea bed, Hawaii's Mauna Kea is taller than Mt Everest by 1,355 m (4,446 ft)

Mount Vesuvius, Italy, 1,277 m (4,190 ft)

EARTHQUAKE RECORDS

EARTHQUAKES are brief, lasting no more than a few minutes, yet they can cause huge casualties in a short time – far worse than most volcanic eruptions – and bring devastation to vast areas. Because they leave none of the dramatic relics that volcanoes do, the record of major earthquakes in the past is scanty.

LEVELS OF DESTRUCTION
Although the Richter scale measures ground movement during a quake, it does not necessarily indicate the degree of destruction. The death toll is more likely to relate to population levels and building methods.

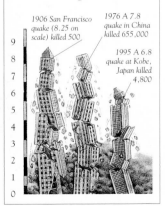

1906 San Francisco quake (8.25 on scale) killed 500

1976 A 7.8 quake in China killed 655,000

1995 A 6.8 quake at Kobe, Japan killed 4,800

• **464 BC** An earthquake in Sparta, Greece, killed 20,000 people.

• **AD 856** An earthquake destroyed the Greek town of Corinth, killing 45,000.

• **1038** 100,000 people were killed by an earthquake in Chihli, China.

• **1293** An earthquake in Kamekura, Japan, killed 30,000.

• **1556** An earthquake of roughly 8.3 on the Richter scale killed over 800,000 people in Shansi, China.

• **1667** An earthquake at Shemaka, the Caucasus, killed over 80,000 people.

• **1731** An earthquake killed 100,000 people in Peking, China.

• **1755** A 9.0 earthquake centred on Lisbon, Portugal, destroyed the city and was felt right across Europe. Over 100,000 people died.

• **1811–1812** Quakes centred on New Madrid, Missouri, reshaped the Mississippi Valley, USA.

• **1906** Tremors and fire virtually destroyed San Francisco.

• **1908** A quake hit Messina in Sicily and Reggio in Calabria, Italy, killing 160,000 people.

• **1920** An 8.6 earthquake demolished the city of Kansu, China, killing 200,000 people.

• **1923** An 8.3 earthquake hit Tokyo. Over 200,000 people died in the resulting firestorm, which was started by overturned stoves.

• **1960** A 9.5 quake in southern Chile, the biggest ever recorded, sent tsunamis right across the Pacific to Japan.

• **1964** A massive 8.4 earthquake, the biggest in the northern hemisphere this century struck Anchorage, Alaska.

• **1970** A 7.8 quake hit Ancash, Peru, killing 66,000 people.

• **1976** Tangshan, China, bore the brunt of this century's most devastating quake. It was directly above the quake's hypocentre, and vibrations destroyed 95 per cent of its high-rise homes, killing about 655,000 people.

• **1989** 62 people died when a 7.1 quake hit San Francisco, collapsing a section of Oakland Bay Bridge; cars were crushed to just 0.5 m (18 in).

• **1994** A quake hit Northridge, Los Angeles, destroying 12,500 buildings, ten bridges, and three major roads.

• **1995** A 6.9 quake southwest of Kobe, Japan, killed 4,800 people and left 300,000 homeless.

• **1998** A massive earthquake hit mountains in Afghanistan, destroying several towns. The region's remoteness and winter weather hampered rescue efforts.

SKOPJE, 1963
The Yugoslavian city of Skopje, built on the site of Scupi, an ancient city destroyed by an earthquake in AD 518, was in turn devastated by a quake in 1963. In among the ruins of a collapsed building was this charred book.

MYTHS AND SUPERSTITIONS

THE AWESOME POWER of volcanoes and earthquakes has long been interpreted by humans as evidence of the work of the gods and mythical beings. Many cultures that have experienced volcanic activity have developed myths and superstitions to account for the powerful forces that can rip apart the Earth's surface.

Bronze figure of Hephaistos, first or second century BC

VOLTAIRE

The French writer Voltaire (1694–1778) wrote about the terrible Lisbon quake of 1755 in his book *Candide*. The destruction shocked Europe, but Voltaire poked fun at religious figures, hinting that God was punishing the city for its immorality. He also mocked Lisbon residents, who blamed foreigners for the disaster.

HEPHAISTOS

According to Greek myth, volcanoes on the island of Lemnos were caused by Hephaistos, the god of fire and metalwork, who set up his forge beneath.

NEPTUNE KNOCKS

Earthquakes are not uncommon in Greece, and the waters of the Aegean are often upset by tsunamis. The ancient Greeks believed that these were caused by the sea god Poseidon (known by the Romans as Neptune) banging angrily on the sea floor with his trident.

HOT-HEADED GODDESS

Pele, the goddess of volcanoes, still inspires fear on the Pacific island of Hawaii. This fire-haired goddess is said to make the volcanoes erupt. When she is angry, she stamps the ground, creating earthquakes before emerging from below riding a wave of lava, screaming curses, and hurling hot rocks.

HOLLOW EARTH

The Earth's interior has fascinated people for centuries. Only last century, the French author Jules Verne (1818–1905) wrote his *Journey to the Centre of the Earth*. French thinker Benoit de Maillet (1656–1738) asserted that burning oil and animal fats trapped in hollows inside the Earth caused volcanoes (see p.110).

SHAKY FROG

Many cultures have believed that the world was carried on the back of a giant. Ancient Hindu myth says it sits on the back of eight giant elephants, but for Mongolians it was a frog, which shook the ground when it stumbled.

Glossary

AA LAVA
A crumbly, lumpy lava, formed when molten rock from lava fountains cools and clots as it falls.

ANDESITE
A type of igneous rock, that is named after the Andes Mountains in South America. It forms from a fairly viscous lava, and is often linked to explosive volcanoes.

ASTHENOSPHERE
The softer part of the Earth's surface layers, between 100 and 220 km (62 and 137 miles) below the surface, just below the rigid lithosphere.

AVALANCHE
A sudden, heavy fall of snow, rock, or ice down the side of a mountain.

BASALT
The most common of all volcanic rocks, basalt is dark and fine-grained. It forms from lavas so runny they often create huge floods.

BATHOLITH
Huge intrusion of igneous rock underground, forming a giant dome-shaped lump.

BLACK SMOKER
Volcanic vent on the sea floor that belches hot fluids. These mix with cold sea water, and turn to black fumes of metal oxides and sulphides.

BLOCK
Large, chunky fragments of old volcanic plug blown out by a volcano during an eruption.

BODY WAVE
Earthquake wave travelling deep underground.

BOMBS
Big blobs of lava thrown out by an erupting volcano, which solidify in various shapes as they cool in mid-air.

BOSS
A finger-shaped intrusion in rock.

CALDERA
Large bowl at the top of the volcano formed by the collapse of the summit into the volcano's magma chamber, and often filled with a lake.

COMPOSITE VOLCANO
Volcano built up from both ash and lava – see Stratovolcano.

CONTACT METAMORPHISM
Small-scale change of rock by heat, due to proximity to magma or lava.

CONTINENTAL DRIFT
The slow movement of the continents around the Earth's surface.

CONVERGENCE ZONE
A region where tectonic plates are colliding.

CORE
The metallic centre of the Earth.

CRATER LAKE
A lake formed in a caldera at the top of a volcanic peak.

CRUST
The Earth's thin shell of solid rock.

DACITE
A volcanic rock that forms from fairly viscous lava, typically found in lava domes.

DIKE
A thin wall of igneous rock underground that forms when magma is injected forcibly into the overlying rock, cracking through existing rock strata.

DIVERGENCE ZONE
A region where tectonic plates pull apart.

EFFUSIVE VOLCANO
A volcano that oozes lava almost continuously.

EPICENTRE
The point on the surface directly above the origin of an earthquake, from which tremors radiate.

EXTRUSIVE IGNEOUS ROCK
Rock formed from lava erupted from volcanoes.

FAULT
A fracture in rock, along which blocks of rock slide past each other.

FISSURE VOLCANO
A volcano in which runny lava oozes out of cracks in the ground.

FLOOD BASALT
A huge plateau formed when basalt lava gushes from a fissure volcano.

FUMAROLE
A small vent on the side of volcanoes that emits thick, often sulphurous gases.

GEYSER
A place where water superheated by hot magma underground spouts into the air.

HOT SPOT
A place where rising columns of hot magma in the Earth's mantle burn through the crust, creating a volcano.

HYDROTHERMAL SYSTEM
Mineral-rich water circulating underground as it is heated by hot magma.

HYDROTHERMAL VENT
A place where mineral rich water heated by hot magma under-ground erupts on to the surface – see also Black smoker.

HYPABYSSAL
Shallow igneous intrusion.

HYPOCENTRE
The origin of an earthquake under the ground, from which all tremors radiate.

IGNEOUS ROCK
Rocks that form as hot magma and lava cools.

INTENSITY
The severity of an earthquake at a particular place – see also Magnitude.

INTRUSION
A place where magma wells up under the ground, and cools to form solid rock without erupting on to the surface.

INTRUSIVE IGNEOUS ROCK
Igneous rock that has solidified beneath the Earth's surface.

ISLAND ARC
Chain of islands formed from volcanoes that erupt along the edge of a subduction zone.

LAHAR
Surging mudflows created by volcanoes when huge quantities of volcanic fragments mix with water.

LASER RANGING
A technique for measuring very slight movements of the continents by bouncing laser beams

off a satellite from
ground stations.

LAVA
Hot, molten rock issuing
from a volcano.

LITHOSPHERE
The rigid top 100 km
(62 miles) or so of the
Earth's surface.

MAGMA
Hot, molten rock from
the Earth's mantle.

MAGMA CHAMBER
The large cavity beneath
a volcano where
magma builds up
before an eruption.

MAGNITUDE
The overall power of
an earthquake, measured
by the size of earthquake
waves on a seismometer.

MANTLE
The 2,300 km
(1,429 miles) thick
zone of the Earth's
interior lying between
the crust and the core.

MERCALLI SCALE
A scale which indicates
an earthquake's intensity
at any one place by
observing its effects.

MESOSPHERE
The little-used term for
the layer of the upper
part of the Earth's

mantle below the
asthenosphere.

METAMORPHIC ROCK
Rock formed by the
transformation of other
rocks by intense heat
and pressure.

MOMENT-MAGNITUDE
A scale for measuring
the size of very big
earthquakes, based on
the amount that rocks
are moved. The bigger
the break in the rock,
the bigger the quake.

NUÉE ARDENTE
Literally, a 'glowing
cloud'. Sometimes used
to describe a pyroclastic
flow, in which the flow
mixes with a cloud of
hot ash.

PAHOEHOE LAVA
A hot, runny lava
that moves freely, in
shallow flows.

PEGMATITE
A coarse-grained igneous
rock which forms as the
last of the magma in an
intrusion crystallizes,
often creating rare gems.

PLATE TECTONICS
A theory that the Earth's
crust is made of many
rigid plates that move
relative to each other.

PLINIAN ERUPTION
The most explosive of all
volcanic eruptions, in
which boiling gases blast
ash and fragments over
50 km (31 miles) high
into the air.

PLUG
A core of solidified
magma that plugs the
neck of a volcano.

PLUME
A rising column of light,
hot magma drifting
upwards through the
Earth's mantle.

PLUTONIC
Deep igneous intrusion.

PYROCLAST
Fragment of volcanic
material blasted apart
during an eruption –
typically from the plug.

PYROCLASTIC FLOW
A flowing avalanche of
hot volcanic ash, cinder,
and pyroclasts.

**RADAR
INTERFEROMETRY**
A technique for
measuring slight
changes in the shape
of the ground from the
interaction of radar
beams beamed at
the ground
from satellites.

REGIONAL METAMORPHISM
Large-scale change of rock as a result of plate collision and mountain building.

RHYOLITE
A fine-grained volcanic rock that forms from the most acidic, sticky magma of all and associated with very explosive volcanoes in subduction zones.

RICHTER SCALE
A measure of earthquake magnitude (0–10), based on the size of shock waves recorded on a seismograph.

RING OF FIRE
An area in the Pacific Ocean, which includes many of the world's most active and violent volcanoes.

SEDIMENTARY ROCK
Rock formed by the settling of tiny rock fragments in water.

SEISMIC GAP
A region in an earthquake zone where there is a lull in activity – making it a likely site for a major quake in the future.

SEISMIC WAVE
A vibration reverberating through the ground in an earthquake.

SEISMOMETER
A device for measuring earthquake waves.

SHIELD VOLCANO
Flattened dome, shield shaped volcanoes that form from runny lava, typically at hot spots.

SILL
A thin flat sheet of igneous rock that forms as magma flows between rock layers.

STRATOVOLCANO
A volcano built up from alternate layers of lava and ash, from successive eruptions.

SUBDUCTION
The process by which one tectonic plate is pushed down into the Earth's interior when two collide.

SUPERPLUME
A gigantic rising column of light, hot magma drifting upwards through the Earth's mantle.

SURFACE WAVE
An earthquake wave travelling near the ground surface.

TECTONICS
The movement of the 20 or so huge plates of rigid lithosphere that make up the Earth's outer shell.

TSUNAMI
Destructive sea wave caused by earthquakes under the ocean.

TRANSCURRENT FAULT
Huge fault in which rocks slip sideways past each other.

TRANSFORM
Zone in which tectonic plates slide horizontally past each other.

VEIN
A place where often large mineral crystals grow from hot volcanic fluids in a crack in the rock.

VENT
The neck of a volcano.

VISCOSITY
How sticky or runny a fluid such as magma is.

XENOLITHS
Fragments of old 'foreign' rock, trapped when magma solidifies. These may be partly metamorphosed by heat and pressure.

Index